DAY

DAY TO DAY

A Short Office Book
for families, schools, and other informal gatherings

Compiled by Brother Kenneth CGA

COLLINS

Collins Liturgical Publications
187 Piccadilly, London W1V 9DA

Collins Liturgical Australia
55 Clarence St Sydney 2000 PO Box 3023 Sydney 2001

First published 1983
© compilation William Collins Sons & Co Ltd 1983

ISBN 0 00 599 746 1

Typographical design Colin Reed
Photoset in Great Britain by
Rowland Phototypesetting Ltd,
Bury St Edmunds, Suffolk
and printed by William Collins Sons & Co Ltd, Glasgow

CONTENTS

Acknowledgements	6
Introduction	7
Using this book	9
Opening sentences (nos 1–17)	11
Penitential prayers (nos 18–23)	13
Opening dialogue (no 24)	15
Profession of Faith (nos 25–26)	15
Kyrie and Our Father (nos 27–31)	16
Responses (nos 32–40)	18
Collects (nos 41–72)	22
Hymns (nos 73–103)	30
Psalms (104–141)	48
Lessons (nos 142–171)	81
Canticles (nos 172–198)	89
General Thanksgiving (no 199)	108
Final Prayers (nos 200–201)	109
Blessings (nos 202–206)	110
Calendar	111
Indexes	
Canticles	115
Hymns: first lines	116
Psalms: first lines	116
Psalms: by number	117
Scripture	118
Subjects and Seasons	119

ACKNOWLEDGEMENTS

Grateful acknowledgement is made for permission to reproduce copyright material as follows:

Bible Societies and Collins Publishers for *Good News Bible*, © American Bible Societies 1976: nos. 145, 146, 154, 155, 159, 161, 168, 171

The Book of Common Prayer is Crown copyright; material from the Prayer Book (some in adapted form) is reproduced with permission.

Geoffrey Chapman, a division of Cassell Publishers, for no 103 from James Quinn SJ, *New Hymns for All Seasons*

The Central Board of Finance, for material from *Alternative Service Book 1980*, © The Central Board of Finance of the Church of England 1980: nos 2–4, 8–13, 15, 18–22, 24, 26, 27–30, 32, 41–47, 49, 51–69, 70–71, 199–206
This book does not reproduce the complete text of any service from the *Alternative Service Book 1980*, nor does it include any service authorised for general use in the Church of England by the General Synod or the Archbishops of Canterbury and York.

Church of Melanesia, no 102

Church of the Province of South Africa: no 179

Collins Publishers and the translators, for material from *The Psalms: a new translation for worship* (*The Liturgical psalter*) © English text 1976, 1977 David L. Frost, John A. Emerton, Andrew A. Macintosh: nos 104–141 (except nos 115, 120, 128, 134), 172

Communities Consultative Council Liturgical Publications: nos 35–38

Community of the Glorious Ascension for nos 48, 178

Darton Longman & Todd and Doubleday Inc, for *Jerusalem Bible* © 1966, 1967, 1968: nos 143, 147, 150, 158, 162, 163

International Consultation on English Texts: nos 25, 174, 177, 185, 186, 193

Joint Liturgical Group, from *Daily Office*: nos 175, 176, 181, 182, 183, 184

Oxford and Cambridge University Presses, for *New English Bible* second edition © 1970: nos 144, 148, 152, 153, 156, 160, 164, 165, 167, 169, 170, 180

National Council of Christian Churches of USA, for *Revised Standard Version of the Bible*: nos 142, 149, 151, 157, 166

Society of St Francis, for material from *The Daily Office-SFF*, published 1981: nos 33, 34, 39, 40, 50, 72, 73, 76, 96, 187, 188, 189, 190, 191, 192, 194–7

Stanbrook Abbey, from *Stanbrook Abbey Hymnal*: nos 82, 85, 92, 95

INTRODUCTION

Human beings are creatures of habit. We all manage to acquire bad habits fairly easily, but we may as easily be programmed into good ones. In children certain habits of hygiene are inculcated by wise parents without too many problems. Most of us by our teens clean our teeth as a matter of habit: in fact it has probably become quite a ritual, the same hand reaching for the toothpaste and toothbrush from the same place in the bathroom, and the action taking place from right to left or from left to right as it always has since as far back as we can remember. Habit includes not just what we do, but the precise way in which we do it. How awful it would be if we had to give our whole minds to every little thing that we had to do each day!

Set ways of doing things are essential for everyday living. And if we believe that praising God is an essential part of life then it follows that our daily praise will develop its own set form. Is praise all that important? That all depends on how you see God.

The God of some believers seems to be rather like a tyrant who has to be cajoled into granting favours to his slaves, but that is not how Jesus taught us to know God. The prayer our Lord gave us begins "Our Father". To Jesus 'Father' has more in keeping with our word 'Dad' than with the stern Victorian paterfamilias always addressed by his offspring as 'Sir'.

Jesus himself, during his life in Palestine, went every sabbath to synagogue, where the regular form of worship included psalms and hymns of adoration. Our own seventeenth century priest-poet, George Herbert, wrote

Seven whole days, not one in seven
 I will praise thee;
In my heart, though not in heaven,
 I can raise thee:
Small it is, in this poor sort,
 to enrol thee:
E'en eternity's too short
 to extol thee.

The whole of creation by its very existence is one great act of worship to its creator. Similarly, though in a much more homely vein, the wagging of a dog's tail at the approach of its master or mistress may be seen as an act of adoration. In our daily worship we are, as it were, wagging our tails for God. And why? Because we love him, and want to love him more and more. We love God because he first loved us. That must mean that we, both as individuals and as a group, matter very much to God. The love of God gives meaning to everything else that we do. Praising God is one way in which we express our love for him.

The love that Jesus had and has for the Father is total. Christians, who are united to Jesus, share in that love and when we worship together we are celebrating in time the eternal love of the Son for the Father, and we do it in the power of the Holy Spirit, who is love.

Throughout the year, by its own calendar, the Church works its way through the most important events in the life of Jesus, culminating in Eastertide. Week by week, the Church is even more selective. Every Sunday it celebrates the Resurrection of Christ and every Friday recalls his saving sufferings. Of course from the point of view of eternity, it is impossible to separate Good Friday from Easter Sunday, but as creatures of time most of us have to do so, and we rely on the Christian year to guide us.

Finally it is important to remember that Christian worship does not just involve those who happen to be present in chapel or church while it is going on. If you switch on Radio One at any time you can be reasonably certain to hear pop of one kind or another. If we could switch into Radio Heaven we would always be involved in worship. Indeed in a sense that is what we are doing in any service: joining with the Church in heaven, with the angels and saints who love God more than we can manage just yet, and who find their total joy in his praises.

Using this book

This book combines the daily Offices (services) of *The Alternative Service Book 1980* with additional material from a variety of sources, so that it can be used for Mattins and Evensong, Prayer at Midday and Night Prayer (usually called Compline) and also provide the basis for Family Services. Most services will probably begin as on p. 15, which also contains the general pattern for any Office.

Whoever is leading the worship should not feel constrained to use only material from these pages. The selection of hymns, Bible readings and prayers given here is limited: in churches or chapels where hymn books are readily available, these can be used in conjunction with this book.

Suggestions are made for the use of the *Psalms* on particular days of a week: for example, nos. 104–8 are marked for use on Sunday, 109–13 for Monday and so on. Psalms which are particularly appropriate for certain days and seasons are marked as such. The last four Psalms given are meant for Night Prayer.

Use one or more Psalms as is thought best, and do not be afraid to choose ones that are not actually suggested for a particular day. On the other hand, beware of the temptation to use only a 'highly filtered residue' of the Psalter. The entire Psalter has in any case here been reduced to a quarter of its length: the Introduction to the Psalms, pp. 48–50 below, suggests ways of praying the Psalms.

New Testament 'Psalms' appear among the Canticles (nos. 172–198).

Hymns and Readings have all been arranged first for the days of the week and thereafter according to the Church's year; those for Night Prayer are given at the end of either section.

The *Canticles* are not set out so specifically, but the Venite, Benedictus and Te Deum are traditionally said at Morning Prayer, the Magnificat at Evensong, and Nunc Dimittis at Compline.

The *Collects* are set out for Mornings and Evenings during the week; various prayers for the Church's year follow, and finally a few extra collects that might be found useful are given. In addition the General Thanksgiving and one or two other prayers appear just before the blessings on p. 110. The usual Responses for Compline are on p. 21, but the whole point of this book is to allow freedom of choice within a common pattern of liturgical worship. There is much to be said for including intercessions and for providing time both for free prayer and for silent prayer before the end of an Office. Acts of penitence would seem best at Night Prayer, but may always preface any Office. They can be found on pp. 13 and 14.

Every item in this book has its own number. The service sheet or hymn board for traditional Night Prayer, for instance, would be set out by numbers like this:

16; 19; 20; 68; 102; 139–141; 165; 186; 29; 30; 39; 50; 204; 205.

Mattins on a Sunday Morning could be:

1; 23; 24; 73; 105; 142; 177; 29; 31; 32; 41; 199; 206.

OPENING SENTENCES

1 Jesus said, I am the resurrection and I am life. If a man has faith in me even though he die, he shall come to life; and no one who is alive and has faith shall ever die. (John 11:25)
Sunday

2 Give thanks to the Lord, and call upon his name; tell the nations all that he has done. (Psalm 105:1)
Monday

3 Jesus said, A new commandment I give to you, that you love one another, as I have loved you. (John 13:34)
Tuesday

4 Jesus said, You will receive power when the Holy Spirit comes upon you; and then you will be my witnesses. (Acts 1:8)
Wednesday

5 Jesus said, I am with you always: to the end of the world. (Matthew 28:20)
Thursday

6 Christ himself bore our sins in his body on the tree, that we might die to sin and live to righteousness. By his wounds we have been healed. (1 Peter 2:24)
Friday

7 When we were baptized into Christ Jesus, we were baptized into his death; so that, as Christ was raised from the dead by the Father's glory, we also might walk in newness of life.
(Romans 6:3.4)
Saturday

8   When the Lord comes, he will bring to light things now hidden in darkness, and will disclose the purposes of the heart.
(1 Corinthians 4:5)
Advent

9   God's love for us was revealed when God sent his only Son into the world, so that we could have life through him.   (1 John 4:9)
Christmas

10 Compassion and forgiveness belong to the Lord our God, though we have rebelled against him.   (Daniel 9:9)
Lent

11 God forbid that I should glory, save in the cross of our Lord Jesus Christ, by whom the world is crucified unto me, and I unto the world.   (Galatians 6:14)
Passiontide

12 Praise be to the God and Father of our Lord Jesus Christ! In his great mercy he has given us new birth into a living hope by the resurrection of Jesus Christ from the dead.   (1 Peter 1:3)
Easter

13 Since we have a great high priest who has passed into the heavens, Jesus the Son of God, let us with confidence draw near to the throne of grace.   (Hebrews 4:14.16)
Ascension

14 God's love has been shed abroad in our hearts through the Holy Spirit he has given us.   (Romans 5:5)
Pentecost

15 Let the nations be glad and sing; for God judges the people with righteousness and governs the nations upon earth.   (Psalm 67:4)
Trinity

16 The Lord Almighty grant us a quiet night and a perfect end.
Night Prayer

17 We are members one of another. Even if you are angry, you must not sin: never let the sun set on your anger, and give no opportunity to the devil. (Ephesians 4:25–27)

Night Prayer

PENITENTIAL PRAYERS

18 Leader We have come together as the family of God in our Father's presence
to offer him praise and thanksgiving,
to hear and receive his holy word,
to bring before him the needs of the world,
to ask his forgiveness of our sins,
and to seek his grace,
that through his Son Jesus Christ
we may give ourselves to his service.

19 Leader If we say we have no sin, we deceive ourselves, and the truth is not in us. If we confess our sins, God is faithful and just, and will forgive us our sins and cleanse us from all unrighteousness.

20 Leader Let us confess our sins to Almighty God.

All Almighty God, our heavenly Father,
we have sinned against you and against our fellow men,
in thought and word and deed,
through negligence, through weakness,
through our own deliberate fault.
We are truly sorry and repent of all our sins.
For the sake of your Son, Jesus Christ, who died for us,
forgive us all that is past;
and grant that we may serve you in newness of life;
to the glory of your name. Amen.

21 **All** Father eternal, giver of light and grace,
we have sinned against you and against our fellow men,
in what we have thought,
in what we have said and done,
through ignorance, through weakness,
through our own deliberate fault.
We have wounded your love,
and marred your image in us.
We are sorry and ashamed,
and repent of all our sins.
For the sake of your Son Jesus Christ, who died for us,
forgive us all that is past;
and lead us out from darkness
to walk as children of light. Amen.

Absolution

22 **Priest** Almighty God, who forgives all who truly repent, have mercy upon you, pardon and deliver you from all your sins, confirm and strengthen you in all goodness, and keep you in life eternal; through Jesus Christ our Lord.
All Amen.

Note: if there is no priest present, prayer no. 68 on p. 29 should be used instead of the absolution.

23 **Leader** Lord, you were sent to heal the contrite.
All Have mercy on us.
Leader Lord, you came to call sinners.
All Have mercy on us.
Leader Lord, you plead for us at the right hand of the Father.
All Have mercy on us.

THE OFFICE BEGINS

24 O Lord, open our lips;
   And our mouth shall proclaim your praise.

   Let us worship the Lord.
   All praise to his Name.

   **Glory to the Father, and to the Son,
      and to the Holy Spirit:
   as it was in the beginning, is now,
      and shall be for ever. Amen.**

   Then follow:
   1. Hymn (see nos 73–103, or use a hymn book)
   2. Psalms: one or more may be chosen (see nos 104–141)
   3. A Lesson from the Bible (see nos 142–171, or read from the Bible)
   4. Canticle (see nos 172–198)
   (5. *Sometimes* A Profession of Faith, see nos 25–26)
   6. Kyrie (nos 27, 29)
   7. Our Father (nos 28, 30)
   8. Response (see nos 32–40)
   9. One or more Collects (see nos 41–72)
   (10. Other prayers and intercessions may be added, e.g. nos 200–201)
   11. Blessing (see nos 202–206)

PROFESSION OF FAITH

25 *The Apostles' Creed*

   **I believe in God, the Father almighty,
   creator of heaven and earth.**

I believe in Jesus Christ, his only Son, our Lord.
He was conceived by the power of the Holy Spirit
and born of the Virgin Mary.
He suffered under Pontius Pilate,
was crucified, died, and was buried.
He descended to the dead.
On the third day he rose again.
He ascended into heaven,
and is seated at the right hand of the Father.
He will come again to judge the living and the dead.

I believe in the Holy Spirit,
the holy catholic Church,
the communion of saints,
the forgiveness of sins,
the resurrection of the body,
and the life everlasting. Amen.

26 This is the faith of the Church.

**We believe and trust in God the Father
who made the world
We believe and trust in his Son
Jesus Christ, who redeemed mankind.
We believe and trust in his Holy Spirit,
who gives life to the people of God.
This is our faith.**

KYRIE AND LORD'S PRAYER

27 Lord, have mercy upon us.
Christ, have mercy upon us.
Lord, have mercy upon us.

28 Our Father, who art in heaven,
   hallowed be thy name;
   thy kingdom come;
   thy will be done;
   on earth as it is in heaven.
   Give us this day our daily bread.
   And forgive us our trespasses,
   as we forgive those who trespass against us.
   And lead us not into temptation;
   but deliver us from evil.
   For thine is the kingdom, the power, and the glory,
   for ever and ever. Amen.

29 Lord, have mercy.
   Lord, have mercy.

   Christ, have mercy.
   Christ, have mercy.

   Lord, have mercy.
   Lord, have mercy.

30 Our Father in heaven,
   hallowed be your name,
   your kingdom come,
   your will be done,
   on earth as in heaven.
   Give us today our daily bread.
   Forgive us our sins
   as we forgive those who sin against us.
   Lead us not into temptation
   but deliver us from evil.
   For the kingdom, the power, and the glory are yours
   now and for ever. Amen.

31 (Caribbean Our Father: this needs to be sung)

   Our Father, who art in heaven,
   Hallowed be thy name;

Thy kingdom come, thy will be done,
Hallowed be thy name;

On the earth, as it is in heaven,
Hallowed be thy name;
Give us this day our daily bread,
Hallowed be thy name.

Forgive us all our trespasses,
Hallowed be thy name,
As we forgive those who trespass against us,
Hallowed be thy name.

And lead us not into temptation,
Hallowed be thy name;
But deliver us fróm all that is evil,
Hallowed be thy name.

For thine is the kingdom, the power and the glory
Hallowed by thy name,
For ever, and for ever and ever,
Hallowed be thy name.

Amen, amen, it shall be so,
Hallowed be thy name;
Amen, amen, it shall be so,
Hallowed be thy name.

RESPONSES

32 Show us your mercy, O Lord;
and grant us your salvation.

O Lord, save the Queen;
and teach her counsellors wisdom.

Let your priests be clothed with righteousness;
and let your servants shout for joy.

O Lord, make your ways known upon the earth;
let all nations acknowledge your saving power.

Give your people the blessing of peace;
and let your glory be over all the world.

Make our hearts clean, O God;
and renew a right spirit within us.

33 Save your people, Lord, and bless your inheritance;
Govern and uphold them, now and always.

Day by day we bless you;
We praise your name for ever.

Keep us today, Lord, from all sin;
Have mercy on us, Lord, have mercy.

Lord, show us your love and mercy;
For we put our trust in you.

In you, Lord, is our hope;
Let us not be confounded at the last.

34 Beloved, let us love one another, for love is of God:
He who loves is born of God, and knows God.

Herein is love, not that we loved God, but that he loved us:
And sent his Son to be the expiation for our sins.

Beloved, if God so loved us, we ought also to love one another.
Where love is, there is God.

To God the Father, who loved us and made us accepted in the Beloved;
to God the Son, who loved us and loosed us from our sins by his own blood;
to God the Holy Spirit, who pours the love of God into our hearts.
To the one true God be all love and all glory
  for time and for eternity. Amen.

35 Jesus Christ, Son of the living God, have mercy on us.
Jesus Christ, Son of the living God, have mercy on us.

You who have vanquished the powers of evil.
Have mercy on us.

Glory to the Father and to the Son and to the Holy Spirit:
Jesus Christ, Son of the living God, have mercy on us.

Purge me from my sin, and I shall be pure;
Wash me, and I shall be clean.

36 Great and wonderful are your deeds, Lord God, the Almighty.
Great and wonderful are your deeds, Lord God, the Almighty.

Who shall not revere and praise your name, for you alone are holy,
Lord God, the Almighty.

Glory to the Father and to the Son and to the Holy Spirit:
Great and wonderful are your deeds Lord God, the Almighty.

Our God is exalted and highly to be praised, alleluia;
He is above all and in all for ever, alleluia.

37 We praise you, O Christ, and we bless you,
For by virtue of your Cross joy has come to the world.

For us you faced temptation, suffering and death,
And in you we are brought to new life.

Jesus Christ, Son of the Living God, have mercy on us.
Holy God, holy and strong, holy immortal, have mercy on us.

38 Blessed be God the Father of our Lord Jesus Christ,
For he has blessed us in Christ Jesus with every spiritual blessing.

He chose us in him before the foundation of the world
That we should be holy and blameless before him.

He destined us in love to be his sons through Jesus Christ
To the praise of his glorious grace.

39 Into your hands, O Lord, I commend my spirit.
Into your hands, O Lord, I commend my spirit.

For you have redeemed me, Lord God of truth.
I commend my spirit.

Glory to the Father, and to the Son, and to the Holy Spirit.
Into your hands, O Lord, I commend my spirit.

Keep me as the apple of your eye.
Hide me under the shadow of your wings.

Save us, O Lord, while waking, and guard us while sleeping; that awake we may watch with Christ, and asleep may rest in peace. *Night Prayer*

40 Into your hands, O Lord, I commend my spirit,
    alleluia, alleluia.
**Into your hands, O Lord, I commend my spirit,
alleluia, alleluia.**

For you have redeemed me, Lord God of truth,
    alleluia, alleluia.

Glory to the Father, and to the Son, and to the Holy Spirit.
**Into your hands, O Lord, I commend my spirit,
alleluia, alleluia.**

Keep me as the apple of your eye, alleluia.
Hide me under the shadow of your wings, alleluia.

Christ is risen, alleluia.
Alleluia, he is risen indeed. *Eastertide*

COLLECTS

Morning

41 Heavenly Father,
whose blessed Son was revealed
    that he might destroy the works of the devil
and make us the sons of God
and heirs of eternal life:
grant that we, having this hope,
may purify ourselves even as he is pure;
that when he shall appear in power and great glory
we may be made like him
    in his eternal and glorious kingdom;
where he is alive and reigns
    with you and the Holy Spirit,
one God, now and for ever.   **Amen**

42 O God,
the author of peace and lover of concord,
to know you is eternal life,
to serve you is perfect freedom.
Defend us your servants from all assaults of our enemies;
that we may trust in your defence,
and not fear the power of any adversaries;
through Jesus Christ our Lord.   **Amen.**

43 Almighty and everlasting Father,
we thank you that you have brought us safely
to the beginning of this day.
Keep us from falling into sin
or running into danger;
order us in all our doings;
and guide us to do always what is right in your eyes;
through Jesus Christ our Lord.   **Amen.**

44 Eternal God and Father,
you create us by your power
and redeem us by your love:
guide and strengthen us by your Spirit,
that we may give ourselves in love and service
to one another and to you;
through Jesus Christ our Lord. **Amen.**

45 Eternal God, the King of Glory,
you have exalted your only Son
with great triumph to your kingdom in heaven.
Leave us not comfortless,
but send your Holy Spirit to strengthen us
and exalt us to the place
where Christ is gone before,
and where with you and the Holy Spirit
he is worshipped and glorified,
now and for ever. **Amen.**

46 Almighty and everlasting God,
who in your tender love towards mankind sent your Son our Saviour Jesus Christ
to take upon him our flesh
and to suffer death upon the cross:
grant that we may follow the example of his patience and humility,
and also be made partakers of his resurrection;
through Jesus Christ our Lord. **Amen.**

47 Grant, Lord,
that we who are baptized into the death of your Son our Saviour Jesus Christ
may continually put to death our evil desires and be buried with him;
that through the grave and gate of death
we may pass to our joyful resurrection;

through his merits, who died and was buried and rose again for us,
your Son Jesus Christ our Lord. **Amen.**

Evening

48 O holy Father, ever-living God,
who, by your Son's journey through the grave,
have made death the gate of heaven;
grant that as we have been buried with him in baptism
so we may wear the likeness of his heavenly manhood;
through the same Jesus Christ our Lord,
who lives and reigns with you and the Holy Spirit,
one God, now and for ever. **Amen.**

49 O God,
the source of all good desires,
all right judgements, and all just works,
give to your servants that peace which the world cannot give;
that our hearts may be set to obey your commandments,
and that freed from fear of our enemies,
we may pass our time in rest and quietness;
through Jesus Christ our Lord. **Amen.**

50 Visit our homes/this place, O Lord we pray,
and drive far away all the snares of the enemy;
may your holy angels dwell with us
    and guard us in peace
and may your blessing be always upon us;
through Jesus Christ our Lord. **Amen.**

51 O Lord,
support us all the day long of this troublous life,
until the shades lengthen, and the evening comes,
and the busy world is hushed,
the fever of life is over,
and our work is done.
Then, Lord, in your mercy grant us safe lodging,
a holy rest, and peace at the last;
through Jesus Christ our Lord. **Amen.**

52 Almighty Father,
whose Son Jesus Christ has taught us
that what we do for the least of our brethren we do also for him:
give us the will to be the servant of others as he was the servant of all,
who gave up his life and died for us,
yet is alive and reigns with you and the Holy Spirit,
one God, now and for ever. **Amen.**

53 Almighty Father,
look with mercy on this your family
for which our Lord Jesus Christ was content to be betrayed
and given up into the hands of wicked men
and to suffer death upon the cross;
who is alive and glorified with you and the Holy Spirit,
one God, now and for ever. **Amen.**

54 Lighten our darkness, Lord, we pray;
and in your mercy defend us from all perils and dangers of this night;
for the love of your only Son,
our Saviour Jesus Christ. **Amen.**

55 Almighty God,
give us grace to cast away the works of darkness
and to put on the armour of light,
now in the time of this mortal life,
in which your Son Jesus Christ came to us in great humility:
so that on the last day,
when he shall come again in his glorious majesty
to judge the living and the dead,
we may rise to the life immortal;
through him who is alive and reigns with you and the Holy Spirit,
one God, now and for ever. **Amen.**   *Advent*

56 All praise to you, Almighty God and heavenly king,
who sent your Son into the world
to take our nature upon him
and to be born of a pure virgin:
grant that, as we are born again in him,
so he may continually dwell in us
and reign on earth as he reigns in heaven
with you and the Holy Spirit
now and for ever. **Amen.** *Christmas*

57 Almighty God,
who anointed Jesus at his baptism with the Holy Spirit
and revealed him as your beloved Son:
inspire us, your children,
who are born of water and the Spirit,
to surrender our lives to your service,
that we may rejoice to be called
   the sons of God;
through Jesus Christ our Lord. **Amen.** *Epiphany*

58 Almighty and everlasting God,
you hate nothing that you have made
and forgive the sins of all those who are penitent.
Create and make in us new and contrite hearts,
that, lamenting our sins
   and acknowledging our wretchedness,
we may receive from you, the God of all mercy,
perfect forgiveness and peace;
through Jesus Christ our Lord. **Amen.** *Lent*

59 Almighty God,
whose most dear Son went not up to joy but first he suffered pain,
and entered not into glory before he was crucified:
mercifully grant that we, walking in the way of the cross,
may find it none other than the way of life and peace;
through Jesus Christ our Lord. **Amen.** *Passiontide*

60 Lord of all life and power,
who through the mighty resurrection of your Son
overcame the old order of sin and death
to make all things new in him:
grant that we, being dead to sin
and alive to you in Jesus Christ,
may reign with him in glory;
to whom with you and the Holy Spirit
be praise and honour, glory and might,
now and in all eternity. **Amen.** *Easter*

61 Almighty God,
as we believe your only-begotten Son our Lord Jesus Christ
  to have ascended into the heavens,
so may we also in heart and mind thither ascend
and with him continually dwell;
who is alive and reigns with you and the Holy Spirit,
one God, now and for ever. **Amen.** *Ascension*

62 Almighty God,
who on the day of Pentecost
sent your Holy Spirit to the disciples
with the wind from heaven and in tongues of flame,
filling them with joy and boldness to preach the gospel:
send us out in the power of the same Spirit
to witness to your truth
and to draw all men to the fire of your love;
through Jesus Christ our Lord. **Amen.** *Whitsun*

63 Almighty and eternal God,
you have revealed yourself as Father, Son, and Holy Spirit,
and live and reign in the perfect unity of love.
Hold us firm in this faith,
that we may know you in all your ways
and evermore rejoice in your eternal glory,
who are three Persons in one God,
now and for ever. **Amen.** *Trinity*

64 Almighty God,
who chose the Blessed Virgin Mary,
to be the mother of your only Son;
grant that we who are redeemed by his blood
may share with her in the glory of your eternal kingdom;
through Jesus Christ our Lord,
who is alive and reigns with you and the Holy Spirit,
one God, now and for ever. **Amen.**

Blessed Virgin Mary

65 Almighty God,
you have built your Church upon the foundation
   of the apostles and prophets
with Jesus Christ himself as the chief corner-stone.
So join us together in unity of spirit by their doctrine
that we may be made a holy temple acceptable to you;
through Jesus Christ our Lord. **Amen.**

Apostle

66 Almighty God,
by whose grace and power your holy *martyr N*
triumphed over suffering and *was* faithful unto death:
strengthen us with your grace,
that we may endure reproach and persecution,
and faithfully bear witness to the name of Jesus Christ our Lord,
who is alive and reigns with you and the Holy Spirit,
one God, now and for ever. **Amen.**

Martyr

67 Almighty God,
you have knit together your elect
into one communion and fellowship in the mystical body of your
   Son.
Give us grace so to follow your blessed saints
in all virtuous and godly living,
that we may come to those unspeakable joys
which you have prepared for those who truly love you;
through Jesus Christ our Lord. **Amen.**

Saint

68 Almighty God,
you have made us for yourself,
and our hearts are restless
till they find their rest in you.
Teach us to offer ourselves to your service,
that here we may have your peace,
and in the world to come may see you face to face;
through Jesus Christ our Lord. **Amen.**

69 Merciful Lord,
grant to your faithful people pardon and peace:
that we may be cleansed from all our sins
and serve you with a quiet mind;
through Jesus Christ our Lord. **Amen.**

70 Merciful God,
you have prepared for those who love you
such good things as pass man's understanding.
Pour into our hearts such love toward you
that we, loving you above all things,
may obtain your promises,
which exceed all that we can desire:
through Jesus Christ our Lord. **Amen.**

71 Stir up, O Lord, the wills of your faithful people;
that richly bearing the fruit of good works,
they may by you be richly rewarded;
through Jesus Christ our Lord. **Amen.**

72 Look down, O Lord,
from your heavenly throne
and illuminate the darkness of this night
    with your celestial brightness,
and from the children of light
banish the deeds of darkness;
through Jesus Christ our Lord. **Amen.**   *Night Prayer*

HYMNS

Mornin[g]

73 Tune GONFALON ROYAL

1 To God our Father, thanks and praise
For this, the first and dawn of days:
The day when through your word of might
From chaos was created light.

2 The day on which your well-loved Son
O'er death and hell the triumph won;
The day on which the Spirit came,
Your gift to men, in wind and flame.

3 To you, our Father, through your Son,
And in the Spirit, Three in One.
We, new-created on this day,
New songs of love and glory pay.

Sunda[y]

74 Tune GRENOBLE

1 O Boundless Wisdom, God most high,
O Maker of the earth and sky,
Who bade the parted waters flow
In heaven above, on earth below:

2 The streams on earth, the clouds in heaven,
By you their ordered bounds were given,
Lest 'neath the untempered fires of day
The parchèd soil should waste away.

3 E'en so on us who seek your face
Pour forth the waters of your grace;

Tunes: All the suggested tunes (apart from GRENOBLE, no 74) are to b[e]
found in *The English Hymnal*. GRENOBLE is in *The BBC Hymn Boo[k]*
Hymns Ancient and Modern Revised, and *With One Voice*. If necessary,
should generally be possible to sing the hymn unaccompanied.

30 HYMNS

Renew the fount of life within,
And quench the wasting fires of sin.

4 To God the Father, God the Son,
And God the Spirit, praise be done;
May Christ the Lord upon us pour
The Spirit's gift for evermore.   *Monday*

75 Tune MORNING HYMN

1 Awake, my soul, and with the sun
Thy daily stage of duty run;
Shake off dull sloth, and joyful rise
To pay thy morning sacrifice.

2 Redeem thy mis-spent time that's past,
Live this day as if 'twere thy last:
Improve thy talent with due care;
For the great Day thyself prepare.

3 Let all thy converse be sincere,
Thy conscience as the noon-day clear;
Think how all-seeing God thy ways
And all thy secret thoughts surveys.

4 Praise God, from whom all blessings flow,
Praise him, all creatures here below,
Praise him above, ye heavenly host,
Praise Father, Son, and Holy Ghost.   *Tuesday*

76 Tune DUKE STREET

1 Come, Holy Spirit, ever One
With God the Father and the Son:
Come swiftly, Fount of grace, and pour
into our hearts your boundless store.

2 With all our strength, with heart and tongue,
By word and deed your praise be sung:
And love light up our mortal frame
Till others catch the living flame.

3 O Father, that we ask be done
  Through Jesus Christ, your only Son,
  Who, with the Spirit, reigns above,
  Three Persons in one God of love.

Wednesday

77 Tune ST BOTOLPH

1 O Christ, our hope, our hearts' desire,
    Redemption's only spring;
  Creator of the world, are you,
    Its Saviour and its King.

2 O may your mighty love prevail
    Our sinful souls to spare;
  O may we come before your throne,
    And find acceptance there!

3 O Christ, you are our present joy,
    Our future great reward;
  Our only glory may it be
    To glory in the Lord.

4 All praise to you, ascended Lord;
    All glory ever be
  To Father, Son, and Holy Ghost,
    Through all eternity.

Thursday

78 Tune RICHMOND

1 Praise to the holiest in the height,
    And in the depth be praise,
  In all his words most wonderful,
    Most sure in all his ways.

2 O loving wisdom of our God!
    When all was sin and shame,
  A second Adam to the fight
    And to the rescue came.

3 O wisest love! that flesh and blood,
    Which did in Adam fail,

    Should strive afresh against their foe,
        Should strive and should prevail;

4 O generous love! that he who smote
      In man for man the foe,
   The double agony in man
      For man should undergo;

5 And in the garden secretly,
      And on the cross on high,
   Should teach his brethren, and inspire
      To suffer and to die.

6 Praise to the holiest in the height,
      And in the depth be praise,
   In all his words most wonderful,
      Most sure in all his ways.

Friday

79 Tune RATISBON

1 Christ, whose glory fills the skies,
      Christ, the true, the only Light,
   Sun of Righteousness, arise,
      Triumph o'er the shades of night;
Dayspring from on high, be near;
Daystar, in my heart appear.

2 Dark and cheerless is the morn
      Unaccompanied by thee;
   Joyless is the day's return,
      Till thy mercy's beams I see;
Till they inward light impart,
Glad my eyes, and warm my heart.

3 Visit then this soul of mine,
      Pierce the gloom of sin and grief;
Fill me, Radiancy Divine,
      Scatter all my unbelief;
More and more thyself display,
Shining to the perfect day.

Saturday

80 Tune MERTON

1. Hark! a herald voice is calling:
   'Christ is near,' it seems to say,
   'cast away the dreams of darkness,
   waken, children of the day!'

2. Wakened by the solemn warning
   let the earth-bound soul arise;
   Christ, her sun, all sloth dispelling
   shines upon the morning skies.

3. Lo, the Lamb so long expected
   comes with pardon down from heaven;
   let us meet him with repentance,
   pray that we may be forgiven.

4. So when love comes forth in judgment,
   debts and doubts and wrongs to clear,
   faithful may he find his servants
   watching till the dawn appear.

Advent

81 Tune BOYCE

1. Christ, whose blood for all men streamed,
   Light that shone ere morning beamed,
   God and God's eternal Son,
   Ever with the Father one;

2. Splendour of the Father's light,
   Star of hope for ever bright,
   Hearken to the prayers that flow
   From your servants here below.

3. Lord, remember, you in love
   Left your throne in Heav'n above
   Man's frail nature to assume
   In the holy Virgin's womb.

4. Let not earth alone rejoice,
   Seas and skies unite their voice

In a new song, to the morn
   When the Lord of life was born.

5 Virgin born all praises be
   Now, and through eternity;
   To the Father, praise be sung,
   And the Spirit, Three in one.   *Christmas*

82 Tune REDHEAD

1 Unto us a Child is given,
   Christ our Saviour brings release;
   Counsellor, Eternal Father,
   God made man and Prince of Peace.

2 Born of Mary, gentle Virgin,
   By the Spirit of the Lord;
   From eternal ages spoken:
   This, the mighty Father's Word.

3 Love and truth in him shall flower,
   From his strength their vigour take.
   Branches that are bare shall blossom;
   Joy that slept begins to wake.

4 Praise the everlasting Father
   And the Word, his only Son;
   Praise them with the Holy Spirit,
   Perfect Trinity in One.   *Christmas*

83 Tune STUTTGART

1 Bethlehem, of noblest cities
   None can once with you compare:
   You alone the Lord from heaven
   Did for us incarnate bear.

2 Fairer than the sun at morning
   Was the star that told his birth;
   To the lands their God announcing,
   Seen in human form on earth.

3 By its peerless beauty guided
  See the eastern kings appear;
  Bowing low, their gifts they offer,
  Gifts of incense, gold and myrrh.

4 Sacred gifts of mystic meaning:
  Frankincense God to disclose,
  Gold the King of Kings proclaiming,
  Myrrh a future tomb foreshows.

5 Jesus, whom the gentiles worshipped
  At your glad epiphany
  Now to you with God the Father
  And the Spirit glory be.   *Epiphany*

84 Tune ANGEL'S SONG (SONG 34)

1 Now is the healing time decreed
  For sins of heart, or word or deed,
  When we in humble fear record
  The wrong that we have done the Lord;

2 Who, always merciful and good,
  Has borne so long our wayward mood,
  Nor cut us off unsparingly
  In our so great iniquity.

3 Therefore with fasting and with prayer,
  Our secret sorrow we declare;
  With all good striving seek his face,
  And lowly hearted plead for grace.

4 Father and Son and Spirit blessed,
  To you be every prayer addressed,
  In threefold Name you are adored,
  From age to age, the only Lord.   *Lent*

85 Tune ST BERNARD

1 O Cross of Christ, immortal tree
  On which our Saviour died,

The world is sheltered by your arms
   That bore the Crucified.

2 From bitter death and barren wood
   The tree of life is made;
   Its branches bear unfailing fruit
   And leaves that never fade.

3 O faithful Cross, you stand unmoved
   While ages run their course:
   Foundation of the universe,
   Creation's binding force.

4 Give glory to the risen Christ
   And to his Cross give praise,
   The sign of God's unfathomed love,
   The hope of all our days.

Passiontide

86 Tune PASSION CHORALE

1 O sacred head, sore wounded,
   Defiled and put to scorn;
   O kingly head, surrounded
   With mocking crown of thorn:
   How dimmed that eye so tender,
   How wan those cheeks appear,
   How overcast the splendour
   That angel hosts revere!

2 Your face is drawn with anguish
   That once did love display.
   In death's grip now you languish,
   Your strength is drained away.
   O you who bore this burden,
   Who felt this bitter pain,
   It was for sinners' pardon
   Which you alone could gain.

3 In your most bitter passion
   O that some share had I!
   With you for my salvation

Upon the Cross to die.
Ah, keep my heart thus moved
To stand your Cross beneath,
To mourn you well-beloved,
Yet thank you for your death.   *Passiontide*

87 Tune ST THOMAS

1 The Lord is risen indeed!
  Now is his work performed:
  Now is the mighty captive freed,
  And death's strong castle stormed.

2 The Lord is risen indeed!
  Then hell has lost his prey;
  With him is risen the ransomed seed
  To reign in endless day.

3 The Lord is risen indeed!
  He lives, to die no more;
  He lives, the sinner's cause to plead,
  Whose curse and shame he bore.   *Easter*

88 Tune SAVANNAH

1 Love's redeeming work is done;
  Fought the fight, the battle won:
  Lo, our Sun's eclipse is o'er!
  Lo, he sets in blood no more!

2 Vain the stone, the watch, the seal,
  Christ has burst the gates of hell;
  Death in vain forbids his rise;
  Christ has opened paradise.

3 Lives again our glorious King;
  Where, O death, is now thy sting?
  Dying once, he all doth save;
  Where thy victory, O grave?

4 Soar we now where Christ has led,
   Following our exalted head;
   Made like him, like him we rise;
   Ours the cross, the grave, the skies.

5 Hail the Lord of earth and heaven!
   Praise to thee by both be given:
   Thee we greet triumphant now;
   Hail, the Resurrection thou! *Easter*

89 Tune ST MAGNUS (NOTTINGHAM)

1 The head that once was crowned with thorns
   Is crowned with glory now:
   A royal diadem adorns
   The mighty victor's brow.

2 The highest place that heaven affords
   Is his, is his by right,
   The King of kings and Lord of lords,
   And heaven's eternal light;

3 The joy of all who dwell above,
   The joy of all below,
   To whom he manifests his love,
   And grants his name to know.

4 To them the cross, with all its shame,
   With all its grace is given:
   Their name an everlasting name,
   Their joy the joy of heaven.

5 They suffer with their Lord below,
   They reign with him above,
   Their profit and their joy to know
   The mystery of his love.

6 The cross he bore is life and health,
   Though shame and death to him;
   His people's hope, his people's wealth,
   Their everlasting theme. *Ascension*

90 Tune VENI CREATOR

1 Come, O creator, Spirit blest,
   And in our souls take up your rest;
   Come with your grace and heavenly aid,
   To fill the hearts which you have made.

2 Great Paraclete, to you we cry,
   O highest gift of God most high,
   O fount of life, O fire of love,
   And sweet anointing from above!

3 You in your sevenfold gifts are known;
   The finger of God's hand we own;
   The promise of the Father you,
   Who does the tongue with pow'r endue.

4 Our senses kindle from above,
   And make our hearts o'erflow with love;
   With patience firm and virtue high
   The weakness of our flesh supply.

5 Drive far from us the foe we dread
   And grant us your true peace instead;
   So shall we not, with you for Guide,
   Turn from the path of life aside.

6 Oh, may you grace on us bestow
   The Father and the Son to know,
   And you, through endless times confess'd,
   Of both th' eternal Spirit blest.

Whitsun

91 Tune SHIPSTON

1 Firmly I believe and truly
   God is three, and God is one;
   And I next acknowledge duly
   Manhood taken by the Son.

2 And I trust and hope most fully
   In that manhood crucified;

And each thought and deed unruly
  Do to death, as he has died.

3 Simply to his grace and wholly
  Light and life and strength belong,
  And I love supremely, solely,
  Him the holy, him the strong.

4 Adoration ay be given,
  With and through the angelic host,
  To the God of earth and heaven,
  Father, Son, and Holy Ghost.

Trinity

92 Tune DEVONSHIRE

1 God, who made the earth and sky
  And the changing sea,
  Clothed his glory in our flesh:
  Man, with men to be.

2 Mary, Virgin filled with light,
  Chosen from our race,
  Bore the Father's only Son
  By the Spirit's grace.

3 He whom nothing can contain,
  No one can compel,
  Bound his timeless Godhead here,
  In our time to dwell.

4 God, our Father, Lord of days,
  And his only Son,
  With the Holy Spirit praise:
  Trinity in One.

Blessed Virgin Mary

93 Tune ALL SAINTS

1 Who are these, like stars appearing,
  These before God's throne who stand?
  Each a golden crown is wearing;
  Who are all this glorious band?

Alleluya, hark! they sing,
Praising loud their heav'nly King.

2 These are they who have contended
For their Saviour's honour long,
Wrestling on till life was ended,
Following not the sinful throng;
These, who well the fight sustained,
Triumph through the Lamb have gained.

3 These your saints have watched and waited,
Offering up to Christ their will,
Soul and body consecrated,
Day and night to serve him still:
Now, in God's most holy place
Blest they stand before his face.

Saints

94 Tune DUNDEE

1 Let saints on earth in concert sing
With those whose work is done;
For all the servants of our King
In earth and heaven are one.

2 One family, we dwell in him,
One Church, above, beneath;
Though now divided by the stream,
The narrow stream of death.

3 One army of the living God,
To his command we bow;
Part of his host has crossed the flood,
And part is crossing now.

4 E'en now to their eternal home
There pass some spirits blest,
While others to the margin come,
Waiting their call to rest.

5 Jesu, be you our constant Guide;
  Then, when the word is given,
  Bid Jordan's narrow stream divide,
  And bring us safe to heaven.   *Saints*

95 Tune WESTMINSTER

1 When God had filled the earth with life
  And blessed it, to increase,
  Then cattle dwelt with creeping things,
  And lion with lamb, at peace.

2 He gave them vast, untrodden lands,
  With plants to be their food;
  Then God saw all that he had made
  And found it very good.

3 Praise God the Father of all life,
  His Son and Spirit blest,
  By whom creation lives and moves,
  In whom it comes to rest.   *Midday*

96 Tune BROCKHAM

1 O God of truth, O Lord of might,
  You order time and change aright
  And send the early morning ray,
  And light the glow of perfect day.

2 Extinguish every sinful fire
  And banish all our ill desire;
  And while you keep the body whole,
  Shed forth your peace upon the soul.

3 O Father, that we ask be done
  Through Jesus Christ your only Son,
  Who, with the Spirit, reigns above,
  Three Persons in one God of love.   *Midday*

Evening

97 Tune TALLIS ORDINAL

1 O Holy Spirit, Lord of Grace,
   Eternal source of love,
   Inflame, we pray, our inmost hearts
   With fire from heaven above.

2 And as you join with holiest bonds
   The Father and the Son,
   So fill your saints with mutual love,
   And link their hearts in one.

3 To God the Father, God the Son,
   And God the Holy Ghost,
   Eternal glory be from man
   And from the angel-host.

98 Tune WAREHAM

1 O God, creation's secret force,
   Yourself unmoved, all motion's source,
   Who from the morn till evening's ray
   Through all its changes guide the day.

2 Grant us, when this short life is past,
   The glorious evening that shall last,
   That by a holy death attained
   Eternal glory may be gained.

3 O Father, that we ask be done
   Through Jesus Christ, your only Son,
   Who, with the Spirit, reigns above,
   Three Persons in one God of love.

99 Tune NUNC DIMITTIS

1 O gladsome light, O grace
   Of God the Father's face,
   The eternal splendour wearing;
   Celestial, holy, blest,

Our Saviour Jesus Christ,
Joyful in thine appearing.

2 Now, ere day fadeth quite,
We see the evening light,
Our wonted hymn outpouring;
Father of might unknown,
Thee, his incarnate Son,
And Holy Spirit adoring.

3 To thee of right belongs
All praise of holy songs,
O Son of God, lifegiver;
Thee, therefore, O Most High,
The world doth glorify,
And shall exalt for ever.

100 Tune TALLIS CANON

1 Glory to thee, my God, this night
For all the blessings of the light;
Keep me, O keep me, King of kings,
Beneath thy own Almighty wings.

2 Forgive me, Lord, for thy dear Son,
The ill that I this day have done,
That with the world, myself, and thee,
I, ere I sleep, at peace may be.

3 Teach me to live, that I may dread
The grave as little as my bed;
Teach me to die, that so I may
Rise glorious at the awful day.

4 Praise God, from whom all blessings flow,
Praise him, all creatures here below,
Praise him above, Angelic host,
Praise Father, Son, and Holy Ghost.

101 Tune EVENTIDE

1 Abide with me; fast falls the eventide;
   The darkness deepens; Lord, with me abide;
   When other helpers fail, and comforts flee,
   Help of the helpless, O abide with me.

2 Swift to its close ebbs out life's little day;
   Earth's joys grow dim, its glories pass away;
   Change and decay in all around I see;
   O thou, who changest not, abide with me.

3 I need thy Presence every passing hour;
   What but thy grace can foil the tempter's power?
   Who like thyself my guide and stay can be?
   Through cloud and sunshine, Lord, abide with me.

4 I fear no foe with thee at hand to bless;
   Ills have no weight, and tears no bitterness;
   Where is death's sting? Where, Grave, thy victory?
   I triumph still, if Thou abide with me.

5 Hold thou thy Cross before my closing eyes;
   Shine through the gloom, and point me to the skies;
   Heaven's morning breaks, and earth's vain shadows flee;
   In life, in death, O Lord, abide with me.

102 Tune MELCOMBE

1 Before the ending of this day,
   Creator of the world, we pray
   That you, with steadfast love, would keep
   Your watch around us while we sleep.

2 From evil dreams defend our sight,
   From fears and terrors of the night;
   Tread under foot our deadly foe
   That we no sinful thought may know.

3. O Father that we ask be done,
   Through Jesus Christ, your only Son;
   And Holy Spirit, by whose breath
   Our souls are raised to life from death.

103 Tune AR HYD Y NOS

1. Day is done, but Love unfailing
   Dwells ever here;
   Shadows fall, but hope, prevailing,
   Calms every fear.
   Loving Father, none forsaking,
   Take our hearts, of Love's own making,
   Watch our sleeping, guard our waking,
   Be always near!

2. Dark descends, but Light unending
   Shines through our night;
   You are with us, ever lending
   New strength to sight;
   One in love, your truth confessing,
   One in hope of heaven's blessing,
   May we see, in love's possessing,
   Love's endless light!

Four further hymns – metrical psalms – will be found at nos 115 (Ps 34), 120 (Ps 42), 128 (Ps 100), 134 (Ps 23).

INTRODUCTION TO THE PSALMS

There is no doubt that King David wrote some of the Psalms in the Bible, but it is equally clear that he could not have written them all. Other psalms are known: for example, there is a collection called the Psalms of Solomon, and the Greek version of the Old Testament, the Septuagint, contains an extra psalm, Psalm 151, which is to this day included in the psalter of Orthodox Christians.

Although unsure who wrote them, and uncertain when, or even about whom they were originally written, we may be quite sure that when Jesus was on earth, the psalms made up a large portion of the Jewish hymn book that was used in both the temple at Jerusalem and in local synagogues.

We know that Jesus went to synagogue every sabbath when he was grown-up and there is every possibility that he went to school as a boy in the local synagogue at Nazareth. He knew the psalter well and at the most awful moment of his life, when he was hanging on the cross, it was to the psalms that his mind and heart turned as he prayed. That terrible cry from the cross, 'My God, my God, why have you forsaken me', is the beginning of Psalm 22. The Evangelists who report the event make a point of telling us that Jesus used the Hebrew words, and not the Aramaic which was his normal everyday speech. Synagogue and temple worship used biblical Hebrew for much of their worship. From this we know that, in his agony, Jesus was at prayer, for he spoke in the language of prayer.

As the psalms provided Jesus with what he needed in his prayer life, so through the centuries the Church, his Body, has found no better words as vehicles of praise. The psalms are prayers hallowed by the very breath of Jesus Christ himself.

But there is another reason for using the psalms. We call them the Psalms of David, and Son of David is one of the titles of Jesus. In the Old Testament, and especially in the psalms the Church searches for truths about Jesus Christ.

In the Acts of the Apostles, St Luke tells how the early Church quoted Psalm 2 as if it was written about Jesus. Peter and John had just been released, having appeared before the authorities to explain how they had healed a cripple at the Beautiful Gate of the Temple. As soon as they were discharged they went back to their friends and told them everything that the chief priests and elders had said. 'When they (that is the church) heard it, they raised their voices as one man and called upon God, "Why did the Gentiles rage and the peoples lay their plots in vain? The kings of the earth took their stand and the rulers made common cause against the Lord and against his Messiah" ' (Acts 4:23–26).

There is an even clearer reference to Jesus in that Psalm. When he was baptised, according to St Mark's report of the event, Jesus heard from heaven a voice saying, 'You are my son': this phrase comes from Psalm 2 and the verse continues, 'this day have I begotten you' (Ps. 2:6). At the time the psalm was written, that may have been a legally effective phrase used when a king, who had no heir, was adopting as his son a man who would eventually succeed to his throne.

There is yet a third significant verse in Psalm 2: 'I the Lord have set my king on Zion, my holy hill' (v. 6). That is exactly what happened. Jesus was set on a cross on the hill of Calvary outside the walls of Zion. Not exactly the place where you might look for a king. But he was crowned.

The psalms are the prayers *of* Jesus; they may be *about* Jesus; they are the prayers still of the Body of Christ.

Looking for Jesus in the psalms is a way of praying them that has been practised for centuries, and is a wonderful means of expressing our love for the Saviour. Perhaps it is better to employ the psalms in this way, so that Jesus Christ remains the centre of our thoughts rather than trying, sometimes in vain, to make the psalms our own personal prayer. They can be that, of course. We can say, and mean:

O God you are my God (Ps. 63:1)

Out of the depths have I called to you, O Lord (Ps. 130:1)

Praise the Lord O my soul and all that is within me praise his holy name (Ps. 103:1) but in all honesty it is a bit difficult to say 'Lord I am not high-minded, I have no proud looks' and mean it. It makes all the difference if we see such words as the words of Jesus. Of him they were and are true.

> At the end of each Psalm, all say
> **Glory to the Father, and to the Son and to the Holy Spirit:**
> **As it was in the beginning, is now, and shall be for ever, Amen.**

PSALMS

104 PSALM 16:8–11) *Sunday*

8 I have set the Lord always before me:
 he is at my right hand, and I shall not fall.

9 Therefore my heart is glad and my spirit rejoices:
 my flesh also shall rest secure.

10 For you will not give me over to the power of death:
 nor suffer your faithful one to see the Pit.

11 You will show me the path of life:
 in your presence is the fulness of joy,
  and from your right hand flow delights for evermore.

Easter

105 PSALM 24

1 The earth is the Lord's and all that is in it:
 the compass of the world and those who dwell therein.

2 For he has founded it upon the seas:
 and established it upon the waters.

3 Who shall ascend the hill of the Lord:
 or who shall stand in his holy place?

4 He that has clean hands and a pure heart:
    who has not set his soul upon idols,
        nor sworn his oath to a lie.

5 He shall receive blessing from the Lord:
    and recompense from the God of his salvation.

6 Of such a kind as this are those who seek him:
    those who seek your face, O God of Jacob.

7 Lift up your heads, O you gates,
        and be lifted up, you everlasting doors:
    and the King of glory shall come in.

8 Who is the King of glory?:
    the Lord, strong and mighty, the Lord mighty in battle.

9 Lift up your heads, O you gates,
    and be lifted up, you everlasting doors:
    and the King of glory shall come in.

10 Who is the King of glory?:
    the Lord of hosts, he is the King of glory.

Ascension

PSALM 61

1 Hear my loud crying, O God:
    and give heed to my prayer.

2 From the ends of the earth I call to you
        when my heart faints:
    O set me on the rock that is higher than I.

3 For you have been my refuge:
    and my strong tower against the enemy.

4 I will dwell in your tent for ever:
    and find shelter in the covering of your wings.

5 For you have heard my vows, O God:
    you have granted the desire of those that fear your name.

6 You will give the king long life:
  and his years shall endure through many generations.

7 He shall dwell before God for ever:
  loving-kindness and truth shall be his guard.

8 So will I ever sing praises to your name:
  while I daily perform my vows.

107 PSALM 93

1 The Lord is King, and has put on robes of glory:
  the Lord has put on his glory,
    he has girded himself with strength.

2 He has made the world so firm:
  that it cannot be moved.

3 Your throne is established from of old:
  you are from everlasting.

4 The floods have lifted up, O Lord,
    the floods have lifted up their voice:
  the floods lift up their pounding.

5 But mightier than the sound of many waters,
    than the mighty waters or the breakers of the sea:
  the Lord on high is mighty.

6 Your decrees are very sure:
  and holiness, O Lord, adorns your house for ever.

108 PSALM 103:1–4.8–17

1 Praise the Lord, O my soul:
  and all that is within me, praise his holy name.

2 Praise the Lord, O my soul:
  and forget not all his benefits,

3 Who forgives all your sin:
  and heals all your infirmities,

4 Who redeems your life from the Pit:
   and crowns you with mercy and compassion.

8 The Lord is full of compassion and mercy:
   slow to anger and of great goodness.

9 He will not always be chiding:
   nor will he keep his anger for ever.

10 He has not dealt with us according to our sins:
   nor rewarded us according to our wickedness.

11 For as the heavens are high above the earth:
   so great is his mercy over those that fear him;

12 As far as the east is from the west:
   so far has he set our sins from us.

13 As a father is tender towards his children:
   so is the Lord tender to those that fear him.

14 For he knows of what we are made:
   he remembers that we are but dust.

15 The days of man are but as grass:
   he flourishes like a flower of the field;

16 When the wind goes over it, it is gone:
   and its place will know it no more.

17 But the merciful goodness of the Lord
       endures for ever and ever towards those that fear him:
   and his righteousness upon their children's children.

109 PSALM 2 *Monday*

1 Why are the nations in tumult:
   and why do the peoples cherish a vain dream?

2 The kings of the earth rise up
       and the rulers conspire together:
   against the Lord and against his anointed, saying,

3 'Let us break their bonds asunder:
let us throw off their chains from us.'

4 He that dwells in heaven shall laugh them to scorn:
the Lord will hold them in derision.

5 Then will he speak to them in his wrath,
and terrify them in his fury:
'I, the Lord, have set up my king on Zion my holy hill.'

6 I will announce the Lord's decree,
that which he has spoken:
'You are my son, this day have I begotten you.

7 'Ask of me,
and I will give you the nations for your inheritance:
the uttermost parts of the earth for your possession.

8 'You shall break them with a rod of iron:
and shatter them in pieces like a potter's vessel.'

9 Now therefore be wise, O kings:
be advised, you that are judges of the earth.

10 Serve the Lord with awe,
and govern yourselves in fear and trembling:
lest he be angry, and you perish in your course.

11 For his wrath is quickly kindled:
blessed are those that turn to him for refuge. *Epiphany*

110 PSALM 29

1 Ascribe to the Lord, you sons of heaven:
ascribe to the Lord glory and might.

2 Ascribe to the Lord the honour due to his name:
O worship the Lord in the beauty of his holiness.

3 The voice of the Lord is upon the waters:
the God of glory thunders,
the Lord upon the great waters.

4 The voice of the Lord is mighty in operation:
 the voice of the Lord is a glorious voice.

5 The voice of the Lord breaks the cedar-trees:
 the Lord breaks in pieces the cedars of Lebanon.

6 He makes them skip like a calf:
 Lebanon and Sirion like a young wild ox.

7 The voice of the Lord divides the lightning-flash:
 the voice of the Lord whirls the sands of the desert,
  the Lord whirls the desert of Kadesh.

8 The voice of the Lord rends the terebinth trees,
  and strips bare the forests:
 in his temple all cry 'Glory.'

9 The Lord sits enthroned above the water-flood:
 the Lord sits enthroned as a king for ever.

10 The Lord will give strength to his people:
 the Lord will give to his people the blessing of peace.

Ascension

111 PSALM 51.1–12

1 Have mercy on me, O God, in your enduring goodness:
 according to the fulness of your compassion
  blot out my offences.

2 Wash me thoroughly from my wickedness:
 and cleanse me from my sin.

3 For I acknowledge my rebellion:
 and my sin is ever before me.

4 Against you only have I sinned
  and done what is evil in your eyes:
 so you will be just in your sentence
  and blameless in your judging.

5 Surely in wickedness I was brought to birth:
 and in sin my mother conceived me.

6 You that desire truth in the inward parts:
O teach me wisdom in the secret places of the heart.

7 Purge me with hyssop, and I shall be clean:
wash me, and I shall be whiter than snow.

8 Make me hear of joy and gladness:
let the bones which you have broken rejoice.

9 Hide your face from my sins:
and blot out all my iniquities.

10 Create in me a clean heart, O God:
and renew a right spirit within me.

11 Do not cast me out from your presence:
do not take your holy spirit from me.

12 O give me the gladness of your help again:
and support me with a willing spirit. *Lent*

112 PSALM 68:1–20

Part 1

1 God shall arise, and his enemies shall be scattered:
those that hate him shall flee before his face.

2 As smoke is dispersed, so shall they be dispersed:
as wax melts before a fire,
  so shall the wicked perish at the presence of God.

3 But the righteous shall be glad and exult before God:
they shall rejoice with gladness.

4 O sing to God, sing praises to his name:
glorify him that rode through the deserts,
  him whose name is the Lord, and exult before him.

5 He is the father of the fatherless,
  he upholds the cause of the widow:
God in his holy dwelling place.

6 He gives the desolate a home to dwell in,
     and brings the prisoners out into prosperity:
   but rebels must dwell in a barren land.

Part 2

7 O God, when you went out before your people:
   when you marched through the wilderness,

8 The earth shook, the heavens poured down water:
   before the God of Sinai, before God, the God of Israel.

9 You showered down a generous rain, O God:
   you prepared the land of your possession
     when it was weary.

10 And there your people settled:
    in the place that your goodness, O God,
      had made ready for the poor.

Part 3

11 The Lord spoke the word, and great was the company
      of those that carried the tidings:
    'Kings with their armies are fleeing, are fleeing away.

12 'Even the women at home may share in the spoil:
    and will you sit idly among the sheepfolds?

13 'There are images of doves
      whose wings are covered with silver:
    and their pinions with shining gold.'

14 When the Almighty scattered kings:
    they were like snow falling upon Mount Zalmon.

15 The mountain of Bashan is a mighty mountain:
    the mountain of Bashan is a mountain of many peaks.

16 O mountains of many peaks, why look so enviously:
    at the mountain where God is pleased to dwell,
      where the Lord will remain for ever?

17 The chariots of God are twice ten thousand,
    and thousands upon thousands:
  the Lord came from Sinai into his holy place.

18 When you ascended the heights,
    you led the enemy captive,
    you received tribute from men:
  but rebels shall not dwell in the presence of God.

19 Blessed be the Lord day by day,
    who bears us as his burden:
  he is the God of our deliverance.

20 God is to us a God who saves:
  by God the Lord do we escape death. *Pentecost*

113 PSALM 89:1–5

1 Lord, I will sing for ever of your loving-kindnesses:
    my mouth shall proclaim your faithfulness
      throughout all generations.

2 I have said of your loving-kindness
    that it is built for ever:
  you have established your faithfulness in the heavens.

3 The Lord said 'I have made a covenant with my chosen:
  I have sworn an oath to my servant David.

4 'I will establish your line for ever:
  and build up your throne for all generations.'

5 Let the heavens praise your wonders, O Lord:
    and let your faithfulness be sung
      in the assembly of the holy ones. *Christmas*

114 PSALM 8 *Tuesday*

1 O Lord our Governor:
  how glorious is your name in all the earth!

2 Your majesty above the heavens is yet recounted:
    by the mouths of babes and sucklings.

3 You have founded a strong defence
        against your adversaries:
    to quell the enemy and the avenger.

4 When I consider your heavens, the work of your fingers:
    the moon and the stars which you have set in order,

5 What is man, that you should be mindful of him:
    or the son of man, that you should care for him?

6 Yet you have made him little less than a god:
    and have crowned him with glory and honour.

7 You have made him the master of your handiwork:
    and have put all things in subjection beneath his feet,

8 All sheep and oxen:
    and all the creatures of the field,

9 The birds of the air and the fish of the sea:
    and everything that moves
        in the pathways of the great waters.

10 O Lord our Governor:
    how glorious is your name in all the earth!

Ascension

15 PSALM 34 (metric)
Tune WILTSHIRE

1 Through all the changing scenes of life,
        In trouble and in joy,
    The praises of my God shall still
        My heart and tongue employ.

2 O magnify the Lord with me,
        With me exalt his name;
    When in distress to him I called,
        He to my rescue came.

3 The hosts of God encamped around
    The dwellings of the just;
  Deliverance he affords to all
    Who on his succour trust.

4 O make but trial of his love,
    Experience will decide
  How blest they are, and only they,
    Who in his truth confide.

5 Fear him, ye saints, and you will then
    Having nothing else to fear;
  Make you his service your delight,
    Your wants shall be his care.

6 To Father, Son, and Holy Ghost,
    The God whom we adore,
  Be glory, as it was, is now,
    And shall be evermore.

116 PSALM 63

1 O God, you are my God:
    eagerly will I seek you.

2 My soul thirsts for you, my flesh longs for you:
    as a dry and thirsty land where no water is.

3 So it was when I beheld you in the sanctuary:
    and saw your power and your glory.

4 For your unchanging goodness is better than life:
    therefore my lips shall praise you.

5 And so I will bless you as long as I live:
    and in your name will I lift my hands on high.

6 My longing shall be satisfied
    as with marrow and fatness:
    my mouth shall praise you with exultant lips.

7 When I remember you upon my bed:
    when I meditate upon you in the night watches,

8 How you have been my helper:
   then I sing for joy in the shadow of your wings,

9 Then my soul clings to you:
   and your right hand upholds me.

10 Those that seek my life are marked for destruction:
   they shall go down to the deep places of the earth.

11 They shall be delivered to the sword:
   they shall be a portion for jackals.

12 The king will rejoice in God,
     and all who take oaths in his name shall glory:
   but the mouths of liars shall be stopped.

Pentecost

17 PSALM 72:1.7–19

1 Give the king your judgement, O God:
  and your righteousness to the son of a king,

7 In his time shall righteousness flourish:
  and abundance of peace, till the moon shall be no more.

8 His dominion shall stretch from sea to sea:
  from the Great River to the ends of the earth.

9 His adversaries shall bow down before him:
  and his enemies shall lick the dust.

10 The kings of Tarshish and of the isles
      shall bring tribute:
    and kings of Sheba and Seba shall offer gifts.

11 All kings shall fall down before him:
   and all nations do him service.

12 He will deliver the needy when they cry:
   and the poor man that has no helper.

13 He will pity the helpless and the needy:
   and save the lives of the poor.

14 He will redeem them from oppression and violence:
   and their blood shall be precious in his sight.

15 Long may he live, and be given of the gold of Sheba:
   may prayer be made for him continually,
     and men bless him every day.

16 Let there be abundance of wheat in the land:
   let it flourish on the tops of the mountains;

17 Let its ears grow fat like the grain of Lebanon:
   and its sheaves thicken like the grass of the field.

18 Let his name live for ever:
   and endure as long as the sun.

19 Let all peoples use his name in blessing:
   and all nations call him blessed. *Christmas and Epiphan*

118 PSALM 113

1 Praise the Lord, O sing praises, you that are his servants:
  O praise the name of the Lord.

2 Let the name of the Lord be blessed:
  from this time forward and for ever.

3 From the rising of the sun to its going down:
  let the name of the Lord be praised.

4 The Lord is exalted over all the nations:
  and his glory is above the heavens.

5 Who can be likened to the Lord our God:
  in heaven or upon the earth,

6 Who has his dwelling so high:
  yet condescends to look on things beneath?

7 He raises the lowly from the dust:
  and lifts the poor from out of the dungheap;

8 He gives them a place among the princes:
  even among the princes of his people.

9 He causes the barren woman to keep house:
  and makes her a joyful mother of children.
    Praise the Lord. *Christmas*

19 PSALM 15 *Wednesday*

1 Lord, who may abide in your tabernacle:
  or who may dwell upon your holy hill?

2 He that leads an uncorrupt life
    and does the thing which is right:
  who speaks the truth from his heart,
    and has not slandered with his tongue;

3 He that has done no evil to his fellow:
  nor vented abuse against his neighbour;

4 In whose eyes the worthless have no honour:
  but he makes much of those that fear the Lord;

5 He that has sworn to his neighbour:
  and will not go back on his oath;

6 He that has not put his money to usury:
  nor taken a bribe against the innocent.

7 He that does these things:
  shall never be overthrown. *Lent*

20 PSALM 42 (metric)
Tune MARTYRDOM

1 As pants the hart for cooling streams
    When heated in the chase,
  So longs my soul, O God, for thee,
    And thy refreshing grace.

2 For thee, my God, the living God,
    My thirsty soul doth pine:
  O when shall I behold thy face,
    Thou Majesty Divine!

3 Why restless, why cast down, my soul?
　　Hope still, and thou shalt sing
　The praise of him who is thy God,
　　Thy health's eternal spring.

4 To Father, Son, and Holy Ghost.
　　The God whom we adore,
　Be glory, as it was, is now,
　　And shall be evermore.

121　PSALM 46

1 God is our refuge and strength:
　a very present help in trouble.

2 Therefore we will not fear, though the earth be moved:
　and though the mountains are shaken
　　in the midst of the sea;

3 Though the waters rage and foam:
　and though the mountains quake at the rising of the sea.

4 There is a river whose streams make glad the city of God:
　the holy dwelling-place of the Most High.

5 God is in the midst of her,
　　therefore she shall not be moved:
　God will help her, and at break of day.

6 The nations make uproar, and the kingdoms are shaken:
　but God has lifted his voice, and the earth shall tremble.

7 *The Lord of hosts is with us:*
　the God of Jacob is our stronghold.

8 Come then and see what the Lord has done:
　what destruction he has brought upon the earth.

9 He makes wars to cease in all the world:
　he breaks the bow and shatters the spear,
　　and burns the chariots in the fire.

10 'Be still, and know that I am God:
    I will be exalted among the nations,
        I will be exalted upon the earth.'

11 *The Lord of hosts is with us:*
   the God of Jacob is our stronghold. *Ascension*

22 PSALM 90:1–4. 12.14–17

1 Lord, you have been our refuge:
    from one generation to another.

2 Before the mountains were born
        or the earth and the world were brought to be:
    from eternity to eternity you are God.

3 You turn man back into dust:
    saying 'Return to dust, you sons of Adam.'

4 For a thousand years in your sight
        are like yesterday passing:
    or like one watch of the night.

12 Teach us so to number our days:
    that we may apply our hearts to wisdom.

14 O satisfy us early with your mercy:
    that all our days we may rejoice and sing.

15 Give us joy for all the days you have afflicted us:
    for the years we have suffered adversity.

16 Show your servants your work:
    and let their children see your glory.

17 May the gracious favour of the Lord our God be upon us:
    prosper the work of our hands,
        O prosper the work of our hands!

23 PSALM 98

1 O sing to the Lord a new song:
    for he has done marvellous things;

2 His right hand and his holy arm:
   they have got him the victory.

3 The Lord has made known his salvation:
   he has revealed his just deliverance
     in the sight of the nations.

4 He has remembered his mercy and faithfulness
     towards the house of Israel:
   and all the ends of the earth
     have seen the salvation of our God.

5 Shout with joy to the Lord, all the earth:
   break into singing and make melody.

6 Make melody to the Lord upon the harp:
   upon the harp and with the sounds of praise.

7 With trumpets and with horns:
   cry out in triumph before the Lord, the king.

8 Let the sea roar, and all that fills it:
   the good earth and those who live upon it.

9 Let the rivers clap their hands:
   and let the mountains ring out together before the Lord;

10 For he comes to judge the earth:
    he shall judge the world with righteousness,
      and the peoples with equity.   *Easter*

124 PSALM 47   *Thursday*

1 O clap your hands, all you peoples:
   and cry aloud to God with shouts of joy.

2 For the Lord Most High is to be feared:
   he is a great King over all the earth.

3 He cast down peoples under us:
   and the nations beneath our feet.

4 He chose us a land for our possession:
   that was the pride of Jacob, whom he loved.

5 God has gone up with the sound of rejoicing:
 and the Lord to the blast of the horn.

6 O sing praises, sing praises to God:
 O sing praises, sing praises to our King.

7 For God is the King of all the earth:
 O praise him in a well-wrought psalm.

8 God has become the King of the nations:
 he has taken his seat upon his holy throne.

9 The princes of the peoples are gathered together:
 with the people of the God of Abraham.

10 For the mighty ones of the earth
  are become the servants of God:
 and he is greatly exalted.   *Ascension*

125 PSALM 67

1 Let God be gracious to us and bless us:
 and make his face shine upon us,

2 That your ways may be known on earth:
 your liberating power among all nations.

3 Let the peoples praise you, O God:
 let all the peoples praise you.

4 Let the nations be glad and sing:
 for you judge the peoples with integrity,
  and govern the nations upon earth.

5 Let the peoples praise you, O God:
 let all the peoples praise you.

6 Then the earth will yield its fruitfulness:
 and God, our God, will bless us.

7 God shall bless us:
 and all the ends of the earth will fear him.   *Christmas*

PSALM 84

1 How lovely is your dwelling-place:
 O Lord God of hosts!

2 My soul has a desire and longing
  to enter the courts of the Lord:
 my heart and my flesh rejoice in the living God.

3 The sparrow has found her a home,
  and the swallow a nest where she may lay her young:
 even your altar, O Lord of hosts, my King and my God.

4 Blessed are those who dwell in your house:
 they will always be praising you.

5 Blessed is the man whose strength is in you:
 in whose heart are the highways to Zion;

6 Who, going through the valley of dryness,
  finds there a spring from which to drink:
 till the autumn rain shall clothe it with blessings.

7 They go from strength to strength:
 they appear, every one of them,
  before the God of gods in Zion.

8 O Lord God of hosts, hear my prayer:
 give ear, O God of Jacob.

9 Behold, O God, him who reigns over us:
 and look upon the face of your anointed.

10 One day in your courts is better than a thousand:
 I would rather stand at the threshold
  of the house of my God
 than dwell in the tents of ungodliness.

11 For the Lord God is a rampart and a shield,
  the Lord gives favour and honour:
 and no good thing will he withhold
  from those who walk in innocence.

12 O Lord God of hosts:
   blessed is the man who puts his trust in you.

127 PSALM 100

1 O shout to the Lord in triumph, all the earth:
   serve the Lord with gladness,
      and come before his face with songs of joy.

2 Know that the Lord he is God:
   it is he who has made us and we are his;
      we are his people and the sheep of his pasture.

3 Come into his gates with thanksgiving,
      and into his courts with praise:
   give thanks to him, and bless his holy name.

4 For the Lord is good, his loving mercy is for ever:
   his faithfulness throughout all generations.

128 PSALM 100 (metric)
Tune OLD 100TH

1 All people that on earth do dwell,
   Sing to the Lord with cheerful voice;
   Him serve with fear, his praise forth tell,
   Come ye before him, and rejoice.

2 The Lord, ye know, is God indeed;
   Without our aid he did us make;
   We are his flock, he doth us feed,
   And for his sheep he doth us take.

3 O enter then his gates with praise,
   Approach with joy his courts unto;
   Praise, laud, and bless his name always,
   For it is seemly so to do.

4 For why? the Lord our God is good;
   His mercy is for ever sure;
   His truth at all times firmly stood,
   And shall from age to age endure.

5 To Father, Son, and Holy Ghost,
  The God whom heav'n and earth adore,
  From men and from the angel-host
  Be praise and glory evermore.

129 PSALM 57 *Friday*

1 Be merciful to me, O God, be merciful:
  for I come to you for shelter;

2 And in the shadow of your wings will I take refuge:
  until these troubles are over-past.

3 I will call to God Most High:
  to the God who will fulfil his purpose for me.

4 He will send from heaven and save me:
  he will send forth his faithfulness and his loving-kindness,
    and rebuke those that would trample me down.

5 For I lie amidst ravening lions:
  men whose teeth are spears and arrows,
    and their tongue a sharpened sword.

6 *Be exalted, O God, above the heavens:*
  and let your glory be over all the earth.

7 They have set a net for my feet, and I am brought low:
  they have dug a pit before me,
    but shall fall into it themselves.

8 My heart is fixed, O God, my heart is fixed:
  I will sing and make melody.

9 Awake my soul, awake lute and harp:
  for I will awaken the morning.

10 I will give you thanks, O Lord, among the peoples:
   I will sing your praise among the nations.

11 For the greatness of your mercy reaches to the heavens:
   and your faithfulness to the clouds.

12 *Be exalted, O God, above the heavens:*
   and let your glory be over all the earth.   Easter

130 PSALM 69:14–23

14 Answer me, O God, in your abundant goodness:
   and with your sure deliverance.

15 Bring me out of the mire, so that I may not sink:
   let me be delivered from my enemies,
      and from the deep waters.

16 Let not the flood overwhelm me
      or the depths swallow me up:
   let not the Pit shut its mouth upon me.

17 Hear me, O Lord, as your loving-kindess is good:
   turn to me, as your compassion is great.

18 Do not hide your face from your servant:
   for I am in trouble – O be swift to answer me!

19 Draw near to me and redeem me:
   O ransom me because of my enemies!

20 You know all their taunts:
   my adversaries are all in your sight.

21 Insults have broken my heart:
   my shame and disgrace are past healing.

22 I looked for someone to have pity on me,
      but there was no man:
   for some to comfort me, but found none.

23 They gave me poison for food:
   and when I was thirsty, they gave me vinegar to drink.
   Passiontide

131 PSALM 88:1–14

1 O Lord my God, I call for help by day:
  and by night also I cry out before you.

2 Let my prayer come into your presence:
    and turn your ear to my loud crying.

3 For my soul is filled with trouble:
    and my life has come even to the brink of the grave.

4 I am reckoned among those that go down to the Pit:
    I am a man that has no help.

5 I lie among the dead,
        like the slain that sleep in the grave:
    whom you remember no more,
        who are cut off from your power.

6 You have laid me in the lowest Pit:
    in darkness and in the watery depths.

7 Your wrath lies heavy upon me:
    and all your waves are brought against me.

8 You have put my friends far from me:
    and made me to be abhorred by them.

9 I am so fast in prison I cannot get free:
    my eyes fail because of my affliction.

10 Lord, I call to you every day:
    I stretch out my hands toward you.

11 Will you work wonders for the dead:
    or will the shades rise up again to praise you?

12 Shall your love be declared in the grave:
    or your faithfulness in the place of destruction?

13 Will your wonders be made known in the dark:
    or your righteousness
        in the land where all things are forgotten?

14 But to you, Lord, will I cry:
    early in the morning my prayer shall come before you.

Passiontide

PSALM 126

1 When the Lord turned again the fortunes of Zion:
   then were we like men restored to life.

2 Then was our mouth filled with laughter:
   and our tongue with singing.

3 Then said they among the heathen:
   'The Lord has done great things for them.'

4 Truly the Lord has done great things for us:
   and therefore we rejoiced.

5 Turn again our fortunes, O Lord:
   as the streams return to the dry south.

6 Those that sow in tears:
   shall reap with songs of joy.

7 He who goes out weeping, bearing the seed:
   shall come again in gladness,
      bringing his sheaves with him.   *Christmas*

PSALM 138

1 I will give you thanks, O Lord, with my whole heart:
   even before the gods will I sing your praises.

2 I will bow down toward your holy temple
      and give thanks to your name:
   because of your faithfulness and your loving-kindness,
      for you have made your name and your word supreme
      over all things.

3 At a time when I called to you, you gave me answer:
   and put new strength within my soul.

4 All the kings of the earth shall praise you, O Lord:
   for they have heard the words of your mouth;

5 And they shall sing of the ways of the Lord:
    that the glory of the Lord is great.

6 For though the Lord is exalted, he looks upon the lowly:
    but he humbles the proud from afar.

7 Though I walk in the midst of danger,
        yet will you preserve my life:
    you will stretch out your hand against the fury of my
        enemies, and your right hand shall save me.

8 The Lord will complete his purpose for me:
    your loving-kindness, O Lord, endures for ever;
        do not forsake the work of your own hands.

Pentecost

134 PSALM 23 (Metric)
Tune CRIMOND

Saturday

1 The Lord's my shepherd, I'll not want;
        He makes me down to lie
    In pastures green; he leadeth me
        The quiet waters by.

2 My soul he doth restore again,
        And me to walk doth make
    Within the paths of righteousness,
        E'en for his own name's sake.

3 Yea, though I walk in death's dark vale,
        Yet will I fear no ill;
    For thou art with me, and thy rod
        And staff me comfort still.

4 My table thou hast furnished
        In presence of my foes;
    My head thou dost with oil anoint,
        And my cup overflows.

5 Goodness and mercy all my life
        Shall surely follow me,
    And in God's house for evermore
        My dwelling-place shall be.

135 PSALM 96

1 O sing to the Lord a new song:
 sing to the Lord, all the earth.

2 Sing to the Lord and bless his holy name:
 proclaim the good news of his salvation from day to day.

3 Declare his glory among the nations:
 and his wonders among all peoples.

4 For great is the Lord, and greatly to be praised:
 he is more to be feared than all gods.

5 As for all the gods of the nations, they are mere idols:
 it is the Lord who made the heavens.

6 Majesty and glory are before him:
 beauty and power are in his sanctuary.

7 Render to the Lord, you families of the nations:
 render to the Lord glory and might.

8 Render to the Lord the honour due to his name:
 bring offerings and come into his courts.

9 O worship the Lord in the beauty of his holiness:
 let the whole earth stand in awe of him.

10 Say among the nations that the Lord is king:
 he has made the world so firm that it can never be moved;
  and he shall judge the peoples with equity.

11 Let the heavens rejoice and let the earth be glad:
 let the sea roar, and all that fills it;

12 Let the fields rejoice, and everything in them:
 then shall all the trees of the wood
  shout with joy before the Lord;

13 For he comes, he comes to judge the earth:
 he shall judge the world with righteousness,
  and the peoples with his truth.   *Epiphany*

136 PSALM 130

1 Out of the depths have I called to you, O Lord:
Lord, hear my voice,

2 O let your ears consider well:
the voice of my supplication.

3 If you, Lord, should note what we do wrong:
who then, O Lord, could stand?

4 But there is forgiveness with you:
so that you shall be feared.

5 I wait for the Lord, my soul waits for him:
and in his word is my hope.

6 My soul looks for the Lord:
more than watchmen for the morning,
more, I say, than watchmen for the morning.

7 O Israel, trust in the Lord,
for with the Lord there is mercy:
and with him is ample redemption.

8 He will redeem Israel:
from the multitude of his sins.

Lent

137 PSALM 145

1 I will exalt you, O God my king:
I will bless your name for ever and ever.

2 Every day will I bless you:
and praise your name for ever and ever.

3 Great is the Lord, and wonderfully worthy to be praised:
his greatness is past searching out.

4 One generation shall praise your works to another:
and declare your mighty acts.

5 As for me, I will be talking
of the glorious splendour of your majesty:
I will tell the story of your marvellous works.

6 Men shall recount the power of your terrible deeds:
  and I will proclaim your greatness.

7 Their lips shall flow
    with the remembrance of your abundant goodness:
  they shall shout for joy at your righteousness.

8 The Lord is gracious and compassionate:
  slow to anger and of great goodness.

9 The Lord is loving to every man:
  and his mercy is over all his works.

10 All creation praises you, O Lord:
   and your faithful servants bless your name.

11 They speak of the glory of your kingdom:
   and tell of your great might,

12 That all mankind may know your mighty acts:
   and the glorious splendour of your kingdom.

13 Your kingdom is an everlasting kingdom:
   and your dominion endures through all generations.

14 The Lord upholds all those who stumble:
   and raises up those that are bowed down.

15 The eyes of all look to you in hope:
   and you give them their food in due season;

16 You open wide your hand:
   and fill all things living with your bounteous gift.

17 The Lord is just in all his ways:
   and faithful in all his dealings.

18 The Lord is near to all who call upon him:
   to all who call upon him in truth.

19 He will fulfil the desire of those that fear him:
   he will hear their cry, and save them.

20 The Lord preserves all those that love him:
   but the wicked he will utterly destroy.

21 My mouth shall speak the praises of the Lord:
   and let all flesh bless his holy name,
       for ever and ever. *Epiphany*

138 PSALM 4 *Night Prayer*

1 Answer me when I call, O God of my righteousness:
   when I was hard-pressed you set me free;
       be gracious to me now and hear my prayer.

2 Sons of men, how long will you turn my glory to
       my shame:
   how long will you love what is worthless
       and seek after lies?

3 Know that the Lord has shown me his wonderful
       kindness:
   when I call to the Lord he will hear me.

4 Tremble, and do no sin:
   commune with your heart upon your bed
       and be still.

5 Offer the sacrifices that are right:
   and put your trust in the Lord.

6 There are many who say 'Who will show us any good?:
   the light of your countenance, O Lord,
       has gone from us.'

7 Yet you have given my heart more gladness:
   than they have when their corn, wine and oil increase.

8 In peace I will lie down and sleep:
   for you alone, Lord, make me dwell in safety. *Compline*

139 PSALM 31:1–5

1 To you, Lord, have I come for shelter:
   let me never be put to shame.

2 O deliver me in your righteousness:
   incline your ear to me and be swift to save me.

3 Be for me a rock of refuge, a fortress to defend me:
　for you are my high rock and my stronghold.

4 Lead me and guide me for your name's sake:
　bring me out of the net that they have secretly laid for me,
　　for you are my strength.

5 Into your hands I commit my spirit:
　you will redeem me, O Lord God of truth.　　　　*Compline*

PSALM 91

1 He who dwells in the shelter of the Most High:
　who abides under the shadow of the Almighty,

2 He will say to the Lord
　　'You are my refuge and my stronghold:
　my God in whom I trust.'

3 For he will deliver you from the snare of the hunter:
　and from the destroying curse.

4 He will cover you with his wings,
　　and you will be safe under his feathers:
　his faithfulness will be your shield and defence.

5 You shall not be afraid of any terror by night:
　or of the arrow that flies by day,

6 Of the pestilence that walks about in darkness:
　or the plague that destroys at noonday.

7 A thousand may fall beside you,
　　and ten thousand at your right hand:
　but you it shall not touch;

8 Your own eyes shall see:
　and look on the reward of the ungodly.

9 The Lord himself is your refuge:
　you have made the Most High your stronghold.

10 Therefore no harm will befall you:
　nor will any scourge come near your tent.

11 For he will command his angels:
   to keep you in all your ways.

12 They will bear you up in their hands:
   lest you dash your foot against a stone.

13 You will tread on the lion and the adder:
   the young lion and the serpent
      you will trample under foot.

14 'He has set his love upon me,
      and therefore I will deliver him:
   I will lift him out of danger,
      because he has known my name.

15 'When he calls upon me I will answer him:
   I will be with him in trouble,
      I will rescue him and bring him to honour.

16 'With long life I will satisfy him:
   and fill him with my salvation.' *Compline*

141 PSALM 134

1 Come bless the Lord, all you servants of the Lord:
   you that by night stand in the house of our God.

2 Lift up your hands toward the holy place
      and bless the Lord:
   may the Lord bless you from Zion,
      the Lord who made heaven and earth. *Compline*

LESSONS

142 Now if Christ is preached as raised from the dead, how can some of you say that there is no resurrection of the dead? But if there is no resurrection of the dead, then Christ has not been raised: if Christ has not been raised, then our preaching is in vain and your faith is in vain. We are even found to be misrepresenting God.

(1 Cor. 15. 12–15a RSV)
Sunday

143 Guard against foul talk; let your words be for the improvement of others, as occasion offers, and do good to your listeners, otherwise you will only be grieving the Holy Spirit of God who has marked you with his seal for you to be set free when the day comes. Never have grudges against others, or lose your temper, or raise your voice to anybody, or call each other names, or allow any sort of spitefulness. Be friends with one another, and be kind, forgiving each other as readily as God forgave you in Christ. (Ephesians 4. 29–32 JB)
Monday

144 'You are my friends, if you do what I command you. I call you servants no longer; a servant does not know what his master is about. I have called you friends, because I have disclosed to you everything that I heard from my Father. You did not choose me: I chose you. I appointed you to go on and bear fruit, fruit that shall last; so that the Father may give you all that you ask in my name. This is my commandment to you: love one another'.

(John 15.14–17 NEB)
Tuesday

145 As they went on their way, a man said to Jesus, 'I will follow you wherever you go'. Jesus said to him, 'Foxes have holes, and birds have nests, but the Son of Man has nowhere to lie down and rest'. He said to another man, 'Follow me'. But the man said, 'Sir, first let me go back and bury my father'. Jesus answered, 'Let the dead bury their own dead. You go and proclaim the Kingdom of God'. Another man said, 'I will follow you, sir; but first let me go and say good-bye to my family'. Jesus said to him, 'Anyone who starts to plough and then keeps looking back is of no use to the Kingdom of God'. (Luke 9. 57–62 GNB)

Wednesday

146 'I was hungry and you fed me, thirsty and you gave me a drink; I was a stranger and you received me into your homes, naked and you clothed me; I was sick and you took care of me, in prison and you visited me'. The righteous will then answer him, 'When, Lord, did we ever see you hungry and feed you, or thirsty and give you a drink? When did we ever see you a stranger and welcome you in our homes, or naked and clothe you? When did we ever see you sick or in prison, and visit you?' The King will reply, 'I tell you, whenever you did this for one of the least important of these brothers of mine, you did it for me!'

(Matthew 25. 34–41 GNB)

Thursday

147 When Jesus had washed their feet and put on his clothes again he went back to the table. 'Do you understand', he said, 'what I have done to you? You call me Master and Lord, and rightly; so I am. If I, then, the Lord and Master have washed your feet, you should wash each other's feet. I have given you an example so that you may copy what I have done to you. I tell you most solemnly, no servant is greater than his master, no messenger is greater than the man who sent him. Now you know this happiness will be yours if you behave accordingly. (John 13. 12–17, JB)

Friday

148 'You must not think that I have come to bring peace to the earth; I have not come to bring peace, but a sword. I have come to set a man against his father, a daughter against her mother, a son's wife against her mother-in-law; and a man will find his enemies under his own roof. No man is worthy of me who cares more for father or mother than for me; no man is worthy of me who cares more for son or daughter; no man is worthy of me who does not take up his cross and walk in my footsteps. By gaining his life a man will lose it; by losing his life for my sake, he will gain it'.

(Matthew 10. 43–39 NEB)
Saturday

149 I saw in the night visions,

> and behold, with the clouds of heaven
> > there came one like a son of man,
> and he came to the Ancient of Days
> > and was presented before him.
> And to him was given dominion
> > and glory and kingdom,
> that all peoples, nations, and languages should serve him;
> his dominion is an everlasting dominion,
> > which shall not pass away,
> and his kingdom one that shall not be destroyed.

(Daniel 7:13–19 RSV)
Advent

150 God's love for us was revealed
when God sent into the world his only Son
so that we could have life through him;
this is the love I mean:
not our love for God,
but God's love for us when he sent his Son
to be the sacrifice that takes our sins away.
My dear people,
since God has loved us so much,
we too should love one another.
No one has ever seen God;
but as long as we love one another
God will live in us
and his love will be complete in us.

(1 John 4:9–12 JB)
Christmas

151 Sing aloud, O daughter of Zion;
  shout, O Israel!
Rejoice and exult with all your heart,
  O daughter of Jerusalem!
The Lord has taken away the judgments against you,
  he has cast out your enemies.
The King of Israel, the Lord, is in your midst;
  you shall fear evil no more. (Zephaniah 3:14–15 RSV)
Epiphany

152 The grace of God has dawned upon the world with healing for all mankind; and by it we are disciplined to renounce godless ways and worldly desires, and to live a life of temperance, honesty, and godliness in the present age, looking forward to the happy fulfilment of our hope when the splendour of our great God and Saviour Christ Jesus will appear. (Titus 2:11–13 NEB)
Epiphany

153 Put on the garments that suit God's chosen people, his own, his beloved: compassion, kindness, humility, gentleness, patience. Be forbearing with one another, and forgiving, where any of you has cause for complaint: you must forgive as the Lord forgave you. To crown all, there must be love, to bind all together and complete the whole. Let Christ's peace be arbiter in your hearts; to this peace you were called as members of a single body.
(Colossians 2:12–15 NEB)
Lent

154 This is a true saying, to be completely accepted and believed: Christ Jesus came into the world to save sinners. I am the worst of them, but God was merciful to me in order that Christ Jesus might show his full patience in dealing with me, the worst of sinners, as an example for all those who would later believe in him and receive eternal life. (1 Timothy 1:15–16 GNB)
Lent

155 Christ himself suffered for you and left you an example, so that you would follow in his steps. He committed no sin, and no one ever heard a lie come from his lips. When he was insulted, he did not answer back with an insult; when he suffered, he did not threaten, but placed his hopes in God, the righteous Judge. Christ himself carried our sins in his body to the cross, so that we might die to sin and live for righteousness. It is by his wounds that you have been healed. (1 Timothy 2:21b–24b GNB)

Passiontide

156 We know that suffering trains us to endure, and endurance brings proofs that we have stood the test, and this proof is the ground of hope. Such a hope is no mockery, because God's love has flooded our inmost heart through the Holy Spirit he has given us. For at the very time when we were still powerless, then Christ died for the wicked. Even for a just man one of us would hardly die, though perhaps for a good man one might actually brave death; but Christ died for us while we were yet sinners, and that is God's own proof of his love towards us.

(Romans 5:4–8 NEB)
Passiontide

157 If we have been united with Christ in a death like his, we shall certainly be united with him in a resurrection like his. We know that our old self was crucified with him so that the sinful body might be destroyed, and we might no longer be enslaved to sin. For he who has died is freed from sin. But if we have died with Christ, we believe that we shall also live with him. For we know that Christ being raised from the dead will never die again; death no longer has dominion over him. The death he died he died to sin, once for all, but the life he lives he lives to God. So you also must consider yourselves dead to sin and alive to God in Christ Jesus.

Let not sin therefore reign in your mortal bodies, to make you obey their passions. Do not yield your members to sin as instruments of wickedness, but yield yourselves to God as men who have been brought from death to life, and your members to God as instruments of righteousness. For sin will have no dominion over you, since you are not under the law but under grace.

(Romans 6:5–14 RSV) *Passiontide*

158 We wish you the grace and peace of God our Father and of the Lord Jesus Christ, who in order to rescue us from this present wicked world sacrificed himself for our sins, in accordance with the will of God our Father, to whom be glory for ever and ever. Amen. (Galatians 1:3–5 JB)

Passiontide

159 I reckon everything as complete loss for the sake of what is so much more valuable, the knowledge of Christ Jesus my Lord. For his sake I have thrown everything away; I consider it all as mere refuse, so that I may gain Christ and be completely united with him. I no longer have a righteousness of my own, the kind that is gained by obeying the Law. I now have the righteousness that is given through faith in Christ, the righteousness that comes from God and is based on faith. All I want is to know Christ and to experience the power of his resurrection, to share in his sufferings and become like him in his death, in the hope that I myself will be raised from death to life. (Philippians 3:8–11 GNB)

Easter

160 It is in Christ that the complete being of the Godhead dwells embodied, and in him you have been brought to completion. Every power and authority in the universe is subject to him as Head. In him also you were circumcised, not in a physical sense, but by being divested of the lower nature; this is Christ's way of circumcision. For in baptism you were buried with him, in baptism also you were raised to life with him through your faith in the active power of God who raised him from the dead.

(Colossians 2:9–12 NEB)

Easter

161 For this reason we have always prayed for you, ever since we heard about you. We ask God to fill you with the knowledge of his will, with all the wisdom and understanding that his Spirit gives. Then you will be able to live as the Lord wants and will always do what pleases him. Your lives will produce all kinds of good deeds, and you will grow in your knowledge of God. May

you be made strong with all the strength which comes from his glorious power, so that you may be able to endure everything with patience. And with joy give thanks to the Father, who has made you fit to have your share of what God has reserved for his people in the kingdom of light. He rescued us from the power of darkness and brought us safe into the kingdom of his dear Son.

(Colossians 1:9b–13 GNB)

Ascension

162 When the kindness and love of God our saviour for mankind were revealed, it was not because he was concerned with any righteous actions we might have done ourselves; it was for no reason except his own compassion that he saved us, by means of the cleansing water of rebirth and by renewing us with the Holy Spirit which he has so generously poured over us through Jesus Christ our saviour. He did this so that we should be justified by his grace, to become heirs looking forward to inheriting eternal life. (Titus 3:4–7 JB)

Pentecost

163 It was then that, filled with joy by the Holy Spirit, he said, 'I bless you, Father, Lord of heaven and of earth, for hiding these things from the learned and the clever and revealing them to mere children. Yes, Father, for that is what it pleased you to do. Everything has been entrusted to me by my Father; and no one knows who the Son is except the Father, and who the Father is except the Son and those to whom the Son chooses to reveal him.' (Luke 10:21–22 JB)

Trinity

164 You are no longer aliens in a foreign land, but fellow-citizens with God's people, members of God's household. You are built upon the foundation laid by the apostles and prophets, and Christ Jesus himself is the foundation-stone. In him the whole building is bonded together and grows into a holy temple in the Lord. (Ephesians 2:19–21 NEB)

Saints

Night Prayer (Compline)

165 His servants shall see the Lamb face to face, and bear his name on their foreheads. There shall be no more night, nor will they need the light of lamp or sun, for the Lord God will give them light; and they shall reign for evermore. (Revelation 22:9.5 NEB)

166 Jesus said: 'Come to me, all who labour and are heavy laden, and I will give you rest. Take my yoke upon you, and learn from me; for I am gentle and lowly in heart, and you will find rest for your souls. For my yoke is easy, and my burden is light.'
(Matthew 11:28–30 RSV)

167 Awake! be on the alert! Your enemy the devil, like a roaring lion, prowls round looking for someone to devour. Stand up to him, firm in faith, and remember that your brother Christians are going through the same kinds of suffering while they are in the world. (1 Peter 5:8–9 NEB)

168 Lord, you are with us!
We are your people; do not abandon us!' (Jeremiah 14:9 GNB)

169 Now to the One who can keep you from falling and set you in the presence of his glory, jubilant and above reproach, to the only God our Saviour, be glory and majesty, might and authority, through Jesus Christ our Lord, before all time, now, and for evermore. Amen. (Jude 1:24–25 NEB)

170 God has not destined us to the terrors of judgement, but to the full attainment of salvation through our Lord Jesus Christ. He died for us so that we, awake or asleep, might live in company with him. (1 Thessalonians 5:9–10 NEB)

171 As it is, however, there still remains for God's people a rest like God's resting on the seventh day. For whoever receives that rest which God promised will rest from his own work, just as God rested from his. Let us, then, do our best to receive that rest, so that no one of us will fail as they did because of their lack of faith.
(Hebrews 4:9–11a GNB)

CANTICLES*

2 VENITE

1 O come, let us sing out to the Lord:
let us shout in triumph to the rock of our salvation.

2 Let us come before his face with thanksgiving:
and cry out to him joyfully in psalms.

3 For the Lord is a great God:
and a great king above all gods.

4 In his hand are the depths of the earth:
and the peaks of the mountains are his also.

5 The sea is his and he made it:
his hands moulded dry land.

6 Come, let us worship and bow down:
and kneel before the Lord our maker.

7 For he is the Lord our God:
we are his people and the sheep of his pasture.

8 If only you would hear his voice today:
for he comes to judge the earth:

9 he shall judge the world with righteousness:
and the peoples with his truth.

Glory to the Father, and to the Son, and to the Holy Spirit;
as it was in the beginning, is now, and shall be for ever.
Amen.   (from Psalms 95 and 96)

Morning Prayer

---

* For those who wish to follow the general pattern of Mattins or Evensong in *The Alternative Service Book 1980*, an indication appears beneath some canticles as to which days and times they are set. Do not allow these suggestions to become a straitjacket.

At the end of each Canticle where it is indicated:

Glory to the Father, and to the Son, and to the Holy Spirit:
as it was in the beginning, is now, and shall be for ever. Amen

173 EASTER ANTHEMS

1 Christ our passover has been sacrificed for us:
   so let us celebrate the feast,

2 Not with the old leaven of corruption and wickedness:
   but with the unleavened bread of sincerity and truth.

3 Christ once raised from the dead dies no more:
   death has no more dominion over him.

4 In dying he died to sin once for all:
   in living he lives to God.

5 See yourselves, therefore, as dead to sin:
   and alive to God in Jesus Christ our Lord.

6 Christ has been raised from the dead:
   the firstfruits of those who sleep.

7 For as by man came death:
   by man has come also the resurrection of the dead;

8 for as in Adam all die:
   even so in Christ shall all be made alive.

Glory   *Eastertide and Saturday Evening*

174 SONG OF ZECHARIAH (BENEDICTUS)

1 Blessèd be the Lord, the God of Israel:
   for he has come to his people and set them free.

2 He has raised up for us a mighty saviour:
   born of the house of his servant David.

3 Through his holy prophets he promised of old:
   that he would save us from our enemies,
     from the hands of all that hate us.

4 He promised to show mercy to our fathers:
   and to remember his holy covenant.

5 This was the oath he swore to our father Abraham:
   to set us free from the hands of our enemies,

6 free to worship him without fear:
   holy and righteous in his sight
      all the days of our life.

7 You, my child, shall be called the prophet of the Most High:
   for you will go before the Lord to prepare his way,

8 To give his people knowledge of salvation:
   by the forgiveness of all their sins.

9 In the tender compassion of our God:
   the dawn from on high shall break upon us,

10 to shine on those who dwell in darkness and the shadow of death:
   and to guide our feet into the way of peace.

   Glory   (Luke 1:68–79)
                                                Morning Prayer

5 SONG OF THE THREE CHILDREN (BENEDICITE)
Full version

1 Bless the Lord all created things:
   sing his praise and exalt him for ever.

2 Bless the Lord you heavens:
   sing his praise and exalt him for ever.

3 Bless the Lord you angels of the Lord,
   bless the Lord all you his hosts:
   bless the Lord you waters above the heavens,
   sing his praise and exalt him for ever.

4 Bless the Lord sun and moon,
   bless the Lord you stars of heaven:
   bless the Lord all rain and dew,
   sing his praise and exalt him for ever.

5 Bless the Lord all winds that blow,
   bless the Lord you fire and heat:
   bless the Lord scorching wind and bitter cold,
   sing his praise and exalt him for ever.

6 Bless the Lord dews and falling snows,
   bless the Lord you nights and days:
   bless the Lord light and darkness,
   sing his praise and exalt him for ever.

7 Bless the Lord frost and cold,
   bless the Lord you ice and snow:
   bless the Lord lightnings and clouds,
   sing his praise and exalt him for ever.

8 O let the earth bless the Lord,
   bless the Lord you mountains and hills:
   bless the Lord all that grows in the ground,
   sing his praise and exalt him for ever.

9 Bless the Lord you springs,
   bless the Lord you seas and rivers:
   bless the Lord you whales and all that swim in the waters,
   sing his praise and exalt him for ever.

10 Bless the Lord all birds of the air,
   bless the Lord you beasts and cattle:
   bless the Lord all men on the earth,
   sing his praise and exalt him for ever.

11 O People of God bless the Lord,
   bless the Lord you priests of the Lord:
   bless the Lord you servants of the Lord,
   sing his praise and exalt him for ever.

   Bless the Lord all men of upright spirit,
   bless the Lord you that are holy and humble in heart:
   bless the Father, the Son and the Holy Spirit,
   sing his praise and exalt him for ever.

   Morning Prayer

76 BENEDICITE Shortened version

1 Bless the Lord all created things:
sing his praise and exalt him for ever.
Bless the Lord all men on earth:
sing his praise and exalt him for ever.

2 O People of God bless the Lord,
bless the Lord you priests of the Lord:
bless the Lord you servants of the Lord,
sing his praise and exalt him for ever.

3 Bless the Lord all men of upright spirit:
bless the Lord you that are holy and humble in heart;
bless the Father, the Son and the Holy Spirit,
sing his praise and exalt him for ever.

Tuesday Morning

77 TE DEUM

1 You are God and we praise you:
you are the Lord and we acclaim you;
2 you are the eternal Father:
all creation worships you.

3 To you all angels, all the powers of heaven:
cherubim and seraphim, sing in endless praise,
4 Holy, holy, holy Lord, God of power and might:
heaven and earth are full of your glory.

5 The glorious company of apostles praise you:
the noble fellowship of prophets praise you:
the white-robed army of martyrs praise you.

6 Throughout the world the holy Church acclaims you:
   Father, of majesty unbounded;
7 your true and only Son, worthy of all worship:
   and the Holy Spirit, advocate and guide.

8 You, Christ, are the King of glory:
the eternal Son of the Father.

9 When you became man to set us free:
   you did not abhor the Virgin's womb.

10 You overcame the sting of death:
   and opened the kingdom of heaven to all believers.

11 You are seated at God's right hand in glory:
   we believe that you will come and be our judge.

12 Come then, Lord, and help your people:
   bought with the price of your own blood,
13 and bring us with your saints:
   to glory everlasting.

The Te Deum may end at this point.

14 Save your people, Lord, and bless your inheritance:
      govern and uphold them now and always.
15 Day by day we bless you:
      we praise your name for ever.

16 Keep us today, Lord, from all sin:
      have mercy on us, Lord, have mercy.
17 Lord, show us your love and mercy:
      for we put our trust in you.
18 In you, Lord, is our hope:
      let us not be confounded at the last.

Morning Prayer

178 SONG OF THE ASCENSION

1 Exalt we the King of Kings:
   and sing praises to our God.

2 For all power is given to you, O Christ:
   heaven and earth are living with your glory.

3 We have seen the Son of Man:
   ascend where he was before.

4 Rejoice with us then all apostles and faithful of old:
   all who are risen and ascended with Christ.

5 Seek we those things above, where our Saviour in triumph:
   sits on the right hand of God the Father.

6 Grant us to hear the great voice saying:
   Come up hither to the clouds of heaven.

7 For our Saviour being lifted up from the earth:
   will draw all men unto himself.

8 O Jesus the Son of God:
   our great High Priest who is passed into heaven.

9 Make intercession for all your people:
   whose life is hid with you in God.

10 You have purged our sins by yourself:
    have mercy on us, O King of saints.

11 Remember your promise and pour upon us:
    the Holy Spirit to comfort and cheer us.

12 You have led captivity captive:
    send down your gifts upon men.

13 For we believe that you are with us:
    even until the end of the world.

   Glory   *Midday Prayer*

79 THE SONG OF CHRIST'S GLORY

1 Christ Jesus was in the form of God:
   but he did not cling to equality with God.

2 He emptied himself, taking the form of a servant:
   and was born in the likeness of men;

3 Being found in human form, he humbled himself:
   and became obedient unto death, even death on a cross.

4 Therefore God has highly exalted him:
   and bestowed on him the name above every name,

5 That at the name of Jesus every knee should bow:
   in heaven and on earth and under the earth;

6 And every tongue confess that Jesus Christ is Lord:
to the glory of God the Father.

Glory

(Philippians 2:5–11)
Thursday Evening

180 THE SONG OF WISDOM

1 The Lord created me at the beginning of his works:
before all else that he had made, long ago.

2 Alone, I was fashioned in times long past:
at the beginning, long before earth itself;

3 When there was yet no ocean was I born:
no springs brimming with water;

4 Before the mountains were settled in their place:
long before the hills was I born.

5 When as yet he had made neither land nor lake:
nor the first clod of earth;

6 When he set the heavens in their place I was there:
when he girdled the ocean with the horizon;

7 When he fixed the canopy of clouds overhead:
and set the springs of ocean firm in their place;

8 When he prescribed its limits for the sea:
and knit together earth's foundations;

9 Then I was at his side each day, his darling and delight:
playing in his presence continually;

10 Playing on the earth when he had finished it:
while my delight was with mankind;

11 Now my sons, listen to me:
listen to instruction and grow wise, do not reject it.

12 Happy is the man who keeps my ways:
happy the man who listens to me;

13 Watching daily at my threshold:
   with his eyes on the doorway;

14 For he who finds me finds life:
   and wins favour with the Lord;

15 While he who finds me not, hurts himself:
   and all who hate me are in love with death.

   Glory   (Proverbs 8:22–36)
                                            Midday Prayer

81 THE SONG OF MOSES AND OF THE LAMB

1 Great and wonderful are your deeds, Lord God the Almighty:
   just and true are your ways, O King of the nations.

2 Who shall not revere and praise your name, O Lord?
   for you alone are holy.

3 All nations shall come and worship in your presence:
   for your just dealings have been revealed.

4 To him who sits on the throne and to the Lamb:
   be praise and honour, glory and might,
      for ever and ever.   Amen.   (Revelation 15:3–4)
                                            Saturday Morning

82 SONG OF THE SAVIOUR

1 Jesus saviour of the world, come to us in your mercy:
   we look to you to save and help us.

2 By your cross and your life laid down you set your people free:
   we look to you to save and help us.

3 When they were ready to perish you saved your disciples:
   we look to you to come to our help.

4 In the greatness of your mercy loose us from our chains:
   forgive the sins of all your people.

5 Make yourself known as our saviour and mighty deliverer:
    save and help us that we may praise you.

6 Come now and dwell with us, Lord Christ Jesus:
    hear our prayer and be with us always.

7 And when you come in your glory:
    make us to be one with you and to share the life of your kingdom.

Friday Morning

183 A SONG OF PRAISE

1 Glory and honour and power are yours by right, O Lord our God:
    for you created all things, and by your will they have their being.

2 Glory and honour and power are yours by right, O Lamb who was slain:
    for by your blood you ransomed men for God,
    from every race and language and nation,
3 to make them a kingdom of priests,
    to stand and serve before our God.

To him who sits on the throne and to the Lamb:
be praise and honour, glory and might, for ever and ever
Amen.   (Revelation 7:9–11.5:9–10)

Friday Evening

184 BLESS THE LORD

1 Bless the Lord the God of our fathers:
    bless his holy and glorious name;
2 bless him in his holy and glorious temple:
    sing his praise and exalt him for ever.
3 Bless him who beholds the depths:
    bless him who sits between the cherubim;
4 bless him on the throne of his kingdom:
    sing his praise and exalt him for ever.

5 Bless him in the heights of heaven:
   sing his praise and exalt him for ever.

   Bless the Father, the Son and the Holy Spirit:
   sing his praise and exalt him for ever.

   (Song of the Three 29–39)
   Tuesday Evening

85 THE SONG OF THE BLESSED VIRGIN MARY (MAGNIFICAT)

1 My soul proclaims the greatness of the Lord:
   my spirit rejoices in God my Saviour;
2 for he has looked with favour on his lowly servant:
   from this day all generations will call me blessed.

3 The Almighty has done great things for me:
   and holy is his Name.
4 He has mercy on those who fear him:
   in every generation.

5 He has shown the strength of his arm:
   he has scattered the proud in their conceit.
6 He has cast down the mighty from their thrones:
   and has lifted up the lowly.
7 He has filled the hungry with good things:
   and the rich he has sent away empty.

8 He has come to the help of his servant Israel:
   for he has remembered his promise of mercy,
9 the promise he made to our fathers:
   to Abraham and his children for ever.

   Glory

   (Luke 1:46–55)
   Evening Prayer

86 THE SONG OF SIMEON (NUNC DIMITTIS)

1 Lord, now you let your servant go in peace:
   your word has been fulfilled;

2 my own eyes have seen the salvation:
   which you have prepared in the sight of every people;

3 a light to reveal you to the nations:
and the glory of your people Israel.

Glory (Luke 2:29–32)
Night Prayer

187 A SONG OF THE LIGHT

1 O joyful Light, from the pure glory of the eternal heavenly Father:
O holy, blessed Jesus Christ!

2 As we come to the setting of the sun:
and see the evening light,

3 We give thanks and praise to the Father, and to the Son:
and to the Holy Spirit of God.

4 Worthy are you at all times to be sung with holy voices:
O Son of God, O Giver of life; and to be glorified through all creation.

Glory *Evening Prayer*

188 A SONG OF REDEMPTION

1 The Father has delivered us from the dominion of darkness:
and transferred us to the kingdom of his beloved Son.

2 In whom we have redemption:
the forgiveness of our sins.

3 He is the image of the invisible God:
the first-born of all creation.

4 For in him all things were created:
in heaven and on earth, visible and invisible.

5 All things were created through him and for him:
he is before all things and in him all things hold together.

6 He is the head of the body, the Church:
he is the beginning, the first-born from the dead.

7 For it pleased God that in him all fulness should dwell:
    and through him all things be reconciled to himself.

    Glory   (Colossians 1:13–20)

189 A SONG OF SALVATION

1 Now that we have been justified through faith:
    we are at peace with God through Jesus Christ our Lord.

2 And so we exult in our hope of the splendour of God:
    and we even exult in the sufferings we endure.

3 For our hope is not in vain:
    because God's love has flooded our inmost hearts
        through the Holy Spirit.

4 When we were still powerless, Christ died for the wicked:
    he died for us while we were still sinners,
        and so God proves his love towards us.

5 We are more than conquerors through him who loved us:
    for nothing can separate us from God's love in Jesus Christ
        our Lord.

    Glory   (Romans 5:1–8; 8:37–39)

190 A SONG OF GOD'S JUDGEMENT

1 We give thanks to you, Lord God almighty,
        ever present and eternal:
    for you have taken your great power
        and begun to reign.

2 The nations raged,
        but the day of your wrath has come:
    and the time for the dead to be judged.

3 The time has come to reward your servants
        the prophets and saints:
    and those who fear your name
        both small and great.

4 Now the salvation of God has come,
  his power and his glorious kingdom:
  now has come the authority of his Christ.

5 For the accuser of our brothers has been thrown down:
  who accuses them day and night before our God.

6 And they have conquered him by the blood of the Lamb:
  and by their word of witness.

7 Rejoice, then, O heaven:
  and you that dwell therein.

  Glory   (Revelation 11:17.18; 12:10–12)

191 A SONG OF THE LAMB

1 Salvation and glory and power belong to our God:
  his judgements are true and just.

2 Praise our God, all you his servants:
  you who fear him, both small and great.

3 The Lord our God, the Almighty, reigns:
  let us rejoice and exult and give him the glory.

4 The marriage of the Lamb has come:
  and his bride has made herself ready.

  To him who sits on the throne and to the Lamb:
  be praise and honour, glory and might,
      for ever and ever.   Amen.   (Revelation 19:1b. 2.5–7)

Monday Evening

192 SONG OF DAVID

1 Blessed are you, O Lord:
  the God of Israel our father, for ever and ever.

2 Yours, Lord, is the greatness, the power,
  the glory, the splendour and the majesty:
  for everything in heaven and on earth is yours.

3 Yours is the kingdom, O Lord:
 and you are exalted as head over all.

4 Riches and honour come from you:
 and you rule over all.

5 In your hands are power and might:
 yours it is to give power and strength to all.

6 And now we give you thanks, our God:
 and praise your glorious name.

Glory (1 Chronicles 29:10–13)

193 GLORIA IN EXCELSIS

1 Glory to God in the highest:
 and peace to his people on earth.

2 Lord God, heavenly King:
 almighty God and Father,
3 we worship you, we give you thanks:
 we praise you for your glory.

4 Lord Jesus Christ, only Son of the Father:
 Lord God, Lamb of God,
5 you take away the sin of the world:
 have mercy on us;
6 you are seated at the right hand of the Father:
 receive our prayer.

7 For you alone are the Holy One:
 you alone are the Lord,
8 you alone are the Most High, Jesus Christ,
 with the Holy Spirit:
 in the glory of God the Father. Amen.

Thursday Morning

194 A SONG OF THE BRIDE

1 I will greatly rejoice in the Lord:
 my soul shall exult in my God.

2 For he has clothed me with the garments of salvation:
   he has covered me with the cloak of integrity,

3 As a bridegroom decks himself with a garland:
   and as a bride adorns herself with her jewels.

4 For as the earth puts forth her blossom:
   and as seeds in the garden spring up.

5 So shall the Lord God make righteousness and praise:
   blossom before all the nations.

6 For Zion's sake, I will not keep silence:
   and for Jerusalem's sake, I will not rest.

7 Until her deliverance shines forth like the sunrise:
   and her salvation as a burning torch.

8 The nations shall see your deliverance:
   and all kings shall see your glory.

9 Then you shall be called by a new name:
   which the mouth of the Lord will give.

10 You shall be a crown of glory in the hand of the Lord:
   and a royal diadem in the hand of your God.

   Glory   (Isaiah 61:10–11.62:1–3)
   Wednesday Evening

195 THE FIRST SONG OF ISAIAH

1 The people who walked in darkness have seen
     a great light:
   those who dwelt in a land of deep darkness,
     upon them the light has dawned.

2 You have increased their joy and given them great gladness:
   they rejoiced before you as with joy at the harvest.

3 For you have shattered the yoke that burdened them:
   the collar that lay heavy on their shoulders.

4 For to us a child is born, and to us a son is given:
   and the government will be upon his shoulder.

5 And his name will be called 'Wonderful, Counsellor, the Mighty God:
   the Everlasting Father, the Prince of Peace.'

6 Of the increase of his government and of peace:
   there will be no end.

7 Upon the throne of David, and over his kingdom:
   to establish and uphold it with justice and righteousness.

8 From this time forth and for evermore:
   the zeal of the Lord of hosts will do this.

   Glory   (Isaiah 9:2–7)

196 SONG OF THE REDEEMED

1 Behold a great multitude:
   which no man could number.

2 From every nation,
      from all tribes and peoples and tongues:
   standing before the throne and before the Lamb;

3 They were clothed in white robes
      and had palms in their hands:
   and they cried out with a loud voice,

4 'Salvation belongs to our God:
   who sits upon the throne,
      and to the Lamb.'

5 These are those who have come out
      of the great tribulation:
   they have washed their robes
      and made them white in the blood of the Lamb.

6 Therefore they stand before the throne of God:
   and serve him day and night within the temple.

7 And he who sits upon the throne:
  will shelter them with his presence.

8 They shall never again feel hunger or thirst:
  the sun shall not strike them
    nor any scorching heat.

9 For the Lamb at the heart of the throne
    will be their Shepherd:
  and he will guide them to springs of living water.

  Glory   (Revelation 7:9–10.14–17)
                                           Monday Morning

197 THE SECOND SONG OF ISAIAH

1 Arise, shine out, for your light has come:
  the glory of the Lord is rising upon you.

2 Though night still covers the earth:
  and darkness the peoples.

3 Above you the Lord now arises:
  and above you his glory appears.

4 The nations come to your light:
  and kings to your dawning brightness.

5 And your gates will lie open continually:
  shut neither by day nor by night.

6 The sons of your oppressors will come to you bowing:
  at your feet shall fall all who despised you.

7 They will call you 'The City of the Lord':
  'Zion of the Holy One of Israel'.

8 The sound of violence shall be heard
    no longer in your land:
  or ruin and devastation within your borders.

9 You will call your walls 'Salvation':
  and your gates 'Praise'.

10 No more will the sun give you daylight:
   nor moonlight shine upon you.

11 But the Lord will be your everlasting light:
   your God will be your splendour.

   Glory   (Isaiah 60:1–3.11.14.18–19)
   Wednesday Morning

198 CANTICLE OF THE SUN

1 All-highest, all powerful, good Lord,
  to you be praise, glory and honour and every blessing:
  To you alone they are due, and no man is worthy to speak
     your name.

2 Be praised, my Lord, in all your creatures,
  especially Brother Sun who makes daytime.
  Through him you give us light:
  he is beautiful, radiant with great splendour,
  and he is a sign that tells, All-Highest, of you.

3 Be praised, my Lord, for Sister Moon and the stars:
  you formed them in the sky,
  bright and precious and beautiful.

4 Be praised, my Lord, for Brother Wind,
  for the air and clouds:
  for fair, and every kind of weather,
  by which you give your creatures food.

5 Be praised, my Lord, for Sister Water:
  she is most useful and humble, lovely and chaste.

6 Be praised, my Lord, for Brother Fire,
  through whom you light up the night for us:
  He is beautiful and jolly, lusty and strong.

7 Be praised, my Lord, for our Mother Earth,
  who keeps us, and feeds us:
  She brings forth fruits of many kinds, with coloured flowers
     and plants as well.

8 Be praised, my Lord, for those who grant pardon
for love of you, and bear with sickness and vexation:
Blessed are those who suffer these things peaceably
because, All-Highest, they will be granted a crown by you.

9 Be praised, my Lord, for our sister, Bodily Death,
whom no living man can escape.
Woe to those who die in mortal sin:
Blessed are those whom she will find
doing your holy will, for to them the second death will do no harm.

10 Bless and praise my Lord:
Thank him, and serve him
in all humility.

(St Francis of Assisi)

GENERAL THANKSGIVING

199 **Almighty God, Father of all mercies,
we your unworthy servants give you most
    humble and hearty thanks
for all your goodness and loving kindness
to us and to all men.
We bless you for our creation, preservation,
    and all the blessings of this life;
but above all for your immeasurable love
in the redemption of the world by our Lord Jesus Christ,
for the means of grace, and for the hope of glory.
And give us, we pray, such a sense of all our mercies
that our hearts may be unfeignedly thankful,
and that we show forth your praise,
not only with our lips but in our lives,
by giving up ourselves to your service,
and by walking before you in holiness
    and righteousness all our days;**

**through Jesus Christ our Lord,
to whom, with you and the Holy Spirit, be all honour and glory,
forever and ever.** Amen.

FINAL PRAYERS

200 Heavenly Father, you have promised through your Son Jesus Christ, that when we meet in his name, and pray according to his mind, he will be among us and will hear our prayer. In your love and wisdom fulfil our desires, and give us your greatest gift, which is to know you, the only true God, and Jesus Christ our Lord; who is alive and reigns with you and the Holy Spirit, one God, now and for ever. **Amen**.

201 Almighty God, you have given us grace at this time with one accord to make our common supplication to you; and you have promised that when two or three are gathered together in your name you will grant their requests. Fulfil now, O Lord, the desires and petitions of your servants as may be most expedient for them, granting us in this world knowledge of your truth, and in the world to come, life everlasting. **Amen**.

BLESSINGS

202 The grace of our Lord Jesus Christ, and the love of God, and the fellowship of the Holy Spirit be with us all evermore. **Amen.**

203 Now to him who is able to do immeasurably more than all we can ask or conceive, by the power which is at work among us, to him be glory in the Church and in Christ Jesus throughout all ages. **Amen**.

204 The Lord be with you.
And also with you.
Let us bless the Lord.
Thanks be to God.
May the souls of the faithful through the mercy of God rest in peace.

205 The Lord bless us and watch over us,
the Lord make his face shine upon us
and be gracious to us,
the Lord look kindly on us
   and give us peace;
and the blessing of God almighty,
the Father, the Son, and the Holy Spirit,
be among us and remain with us always. **Amen.**

206 The love of the Lord Jesus
draw us to himself,
the power of the Lord Jesus
strengthen us in his service,
the joy of the Lord Jesus fill our hearts;
and the blessing of God almighty,
the Father, the Son, and the Holy Spirit,
be among us and remain with us always. **Amen.**

CALENDAR

JANUARY
- **1** NAMING OF JESUS
- **6** EPIPHANY
- **13** Hilary, bishop of Poitiers 367
- **17** Anthony of Egypt, Abbot 356
- **21** Agnes, virgin martyr 309
- **24** Francis de Sales, bishop 1662
- **25** CONVERSION OF ST PAUL
- **26** **Timothy and Titus, companions of St Paul**
- **27** John Chrysostom, bishop of Constantinople 407
- **28** Thomas Aquinas, priest, teacher of the faith 1274
- **30** Charles I, king and martyr 1649

FEBRUARY
- **2** PRESENTATION OF CHRIST IN THE TEMPLE
- **3** **Saints and martyrs of Europe**
- **4** Gilbert of Sempringham, abbot 1189
- **10** Scholastica, abbess 543
- **14** Valentine, bishop and martyr 270
- **21** **Saints and martyrs of Africa**
- **23** Polycarp, bishop and martyr c. 155
- **27** George Herbert, priest 1633

MARCH
- **1** **David of Wales, bishop c. 601**
- **2** Chad, bishop of Lichfield 672
- **7** Perpetua and her companion, martyrs, Carthage 203
- **8** Edward King, bishop of Lincoln 1910
- **17** **Patrick of Ireland, bishop** c. 460
- **19** JOSEPH OF NAZARETH, HUSBAND OF THE BLESSED VIRGIN MARY
- **20** Cuthbert, bishop of Lindisfarne 687
  Thomas Ken, bishop of Bath and Wells 1711
- **21** Thomas Cranmer, Archbishop of Canterbury, martyr 1556
- **25** ANNUNCIATION OF THE BLESSED VIRGIN MARY
- **29** John Keble, priest 1866

APRIL
- **3** Richard of Chichester, bishop 1253
- **8** **Saints and martyrs of the Americas**
- **9** William Law, mystic 1761
- **21** Anselm, archbishop of Canterbury 1109

APRIL *continued*
- **23 George of England, martyr** 4th century
- 25 MARK THE EVANGELIST
- 29 Catherine of Siena, mystic 1380

MAY
- 1 PHILIP AND JAMES, APOSTLES
- 8 Julian of Norwich, mystic *c.* 1417
- 14 MATTHIAS THE APOSTLE
- 19 Dunstan, archbishop of Canterbury 988
- 25 Venerable Bede of Jarrow, bishop 605
- **26 Augustine of Canterbury, bishop** 605
- 29 John and Charles Wesley 1791, 1788
- **31 Visitation of the Blessed Virgin Mary**

JUNE
- 1 Justin, martyr, Rome *c.* 165
- 5 Boniface, bishop and missionary, martyr 754
- 9 Columba, abbot of Iona, missionary 597
- 11 BARNABAS THE APOSTLE
- 14 Basil the Great 379 and **Fathers of the Eastern Church**
- 22 **Alban, first martyr in Britain** *c.* 209
- 24 NATIVITY OF JOHN THE BAPTIST
- 28 Irenaeus, bishop and martyr *c.* 300
- 29 PETER AND PAUL, APOSTLES

JULY
- 3 THOMAS THE APOSTLE
- 6 Thomas More, martyr 1535
- 11 Benedict, abbot *c.* 550
- 22 MARY MAGDALEN
- 25 JAMES THE GREATER, Apostle
- 26 Anne, Mother of the Blessed Virgin Mary
- 29 William Wilberforce, Social Reformer 1833
- 31 Ignatius Loyola, priest 1556

AUGUST
- 4 Dominic, priest and friar 1221
- 5 Oswald, king of Northumbria, martyr 642
- 6 TRANSFIGURATION OF OUR LORD
- 10 Laurence, Deacon, martyr 258
- 11 Clare of Assisi, virgin 1253
- 15 FALLING ASLEEP OF THE BLESSED VIRGIN MARY
- 20 Bernard of Clairvaux, abbot 1153
- 24 BARTHOLOMEW THE APOSTLE

AUGUST *continued*
- **28** Augustine of Hippo, bishop and teacher of the Church 430
- **29** Beheading of John the Baptist
- **31** Aidan, bishop of Lindisfarne 651
  John Bunyan 1688

SEPTEMBER
- **3** Gregory the Great, bishop and teacher 604
- **8** NATIVITY OF THE BLESSED VIRGIN MARY
- **14** **Triumph of the Cross**
- **20** **John Coleridge Patteson, bishop and martyr 1871**
  Saints and martyrs of Australia and the Pacific
- **21** MATTHEW THE EVANGELIST
- **27** Vincent de Paul, priest 1660
- **25** Launcelot Andrewes, bishop of Winchester 1626
- **29** MICHAEL and ALL ANGELS

OCTOBER
- **4** Francis of Assisi 1226
- **6** Faith, virgin and martyr *c.* 304
  William Tyndale 1536
- **10** Paulinus, bishop 644
- **13** Edward the Confessor, king 1066
- **15** Teresa of Avila, abbess and mystic 1582
- **18** LUKE THE EVANGELIST
- **17** Ignatius of Antioch, bishop and martyr *c.* 107
- **28** SIMON AND JUDE, Apostles
- **29** James Hannington, bishop of East Equatorial Africa, martyr 1805
- **31** Saints and martyrs of the Reformation Era

NOVEMBER
- **1** ALL SAINTS' DAY
- **2** All Souls' Day
- **3** Richard Hooker, teacher of the Church 1600
- **8** **Saints and martyrs of England**
- **11** Martin of Tours, bishop 397
- **13** Charles Simeon, priest 1836
- **16** Margaret of Scotland, queen 1093
- **17** Hilda of Whitby, abbess 680
  Hugh of Lincoln, bishop 1200
- **29** Edmund of East Anglia, king and martyr 870
- **30** ANDREW THE APOSTLE

DECEMBER

- **2** Nicholas Ferrar, deacon, founder of Little Gidding Community 1637
- **3 Francis Xavier, missionary 1552, and Saints and martyrs of Asia**
- **6 Nicholas, bishop of Myra** *c.* 326
- **7** Ambrose of Milan, bishop 397
- **8 Conception of the Blessed Virgin Mary**
- **14** John of the Cross, mystic 1591
- **25** CHRISTMAS DAY
- **26** STEPHEN, THE FIRST MARTYR
- **27** JOHN THE EVANGELIST
- **28** HOLY INNOCENTS
- **29** Thomas Becket, archbishop of Canterbury, martyr 1170
- **30** Josephine Butler, social reformer 1907
- **31** John Wyclif, reformer 1384

INDEXES*

CANTICLES

All-highest, all powerful good Lord	198
Arise, shine out, for your light has come	197
Behold a great multitude	196
Benedicite	175
Benedicite (shortened version)	176
Benedictus	174
Blessed are you	192
Blessed be the Lord the God of Israel	174
Bless the Lord all created things	175
Bless the Lord all created things (shortened version)	176
Bless the Lord the God of our fathers	184
Cantate Domino	123
Canticle of the Sun	198
Christ our Passover	173
Christ Jesus was in the form of God	179
Deus Misereatur	125
Easter Anthems	173
Exalt we the King of Kings	178
Gloria in Excelsis	193
Glory and honour and power	183
Glory to God in the highest	193
Great and wonderful are your deeds	181
I will greatly rejoice in the Lord	194
Jesus Saviour of the world	182
Jubilate	127
Lord now you let your servant	186
Magnificat	185
My soul proclaims the greatness	185
Now that we have been justified	189
Nunc Dimittis	172
O come let us sing out to the Lord	172
O joyful light	187
Salvation and glory and power	191
Saviour of the world	
Second Song of Isaiah	197
Song of Ascension	178
Song of Christ's Glory	179
Song of David	192
Song of God's Judgment	190
Song of Isaiah	195
Song of Moses and the Lamb	181
Song of Praise	183
Song of the Redeemed	196
Song of Redemption	188
Song of Salvation	189
Song of Simeon	186
Song of the Blessed Virgin Mary	185
Song of the Bride	194
Song of the Lamb	191
Song of the Light	187
Song of the Saviour	182
Song of the Three	184
Song of Wisdom	180
Te Deum	177
The Father has delivered us	188
The Lord created me at the beginning	180
The people who walked in darkness	195
Venite	172
We give thanks to you Lord God	190
You are God, we praise you	177

* All references in indexes are to item number

HYMNS

Abide with me	101
All people that on earth do dwell	128
As pants the hart for cooling streams	120
Awake my soul and with the sun	75
Before the ending of the day	102
Bethlehem of noblest cities	83
Christ whose blood for all men streamed	81
Christ whose glory fills the sky	79
Come, Holy Spirit, ever One	76
Come, O Creator, Spirit blest	90
Day is done but love unfailing	103
Firmly I believe and truly	91
Glory to thee, my God this night	100
God who made the earth and sky	92
Hark! a herald voice is calling	80
Let saints on earth in concert sing	94
Love's redeeming work is done	88
Now is the healing time decreed	84
O boundless wisdom, God most high	74
O Christ our hope, our hearts' desire	77
O Cross of Christ, immortal tree	85
O gladsome light, O grace	99
O God, creation's secret force	97
O God of Truth, O Lord of might	96
O Holy Spirit, Lord of Grace	98
O Sacred Head sore wounded	86
Praise to the Holiest	78
The head that once was crowned	89
The Lord is risen indeed	87
The Lord's my shepherd	134
To God our Father thanks and praise	73
Through all the changing scenes	115
Unto us a Child is given	82
When God had filled the earth with life	95
Who are these like stars appearing	93

PSALMS (by first line)

All people that on earth do dwell	128
Answer me, O God, in your abundant goodness	130
Answer me when I call, O God of my righteousness	138
Ascribe to the Lord, you Sons of heaven	110
As pants the hart for cooling streams	120
Be merciful to me O God	129
Come bless the Lord, all you servants of the Lord	141
Give the king your judgement, O God	117
God is our refuge and strength	121
God shall arise, and his enemies shall be scattered	112
Have mercy on me, O God	111
Hear my loud crying, O God	106
He who dwells in the shelter of the Most High	140
How lovely is your dwelling-place	126
I have set the Lord always before me	104

I will exalt you, O God my king	137
I will give you thanks, O Lord, with my whole heart	133
Let God be gracious and bless us	125
Lord, I will sing for ever of your loving kindnesses	113
Lord, who may abide in your tabernacle	119
Lord, you have been our refuge	122
O clap your hands, all you peoples	124
O God, you are my God	116
O Lord my God, I call for help by day	131
O Lord our governor	114
O shout to the Lord in triumph	127
O sing to the Lord a new song	123
O sing to the Lord a new song, sing to the Lord all the earth	135
Out of the depths have I called to you, O Lord	136
Praise the Lord, O my soul	108
Praise the Lord, O sing praises	118
The earth is the Lord's	105
The Lord is King and has put on robes of glory	107
The Lord's my shepherd	134
Through all the changing scenes of life	115
To you Lord have I come for shelter	139
When the Lord turned again the fortunes of Zion	132
Why are the nations in tumult	109

PSALMS (by number)

Psalm 2	109	Psalm 72:1.7–19	117
Psalm 4	138	Psalm 84	126
Psalm 8	114	Psalm 88:1–14	131
Psalm 15	119	Psalm 89:1–5	113
Psalm 16:8–11	104	Psalm 90:1–5.12.14–17	122
Psalm 23 (metrical)	134	Psalm 91	140
Psalm 24	105	Psalm 93	107
Psalm 29	110	Psalm 95	172
Psalm 31:1–5	139	Psalm 96	135
Psalm 34 (metrical)	115	Psalm 98	123
Psalm 42 (metrical)	120	Psalm 100	127
Psalm 46	121	Psalm 100 (metrical)	128
Psalm 47	124	Psalm 103:1–4.8–17	108
Psalm 51:1–12	111	Psalm 113	118
Psalm 57	129	Psalm 126	132
Psalm 61	106	Psalm 130	136
Psalm 63	116	Psalm 134	141
Psalm 67	125	Psalm 138	133
Psalm 68:1–20	112	Psalm 145	137
Psalm 69:14–23	130		

SCRIPTURE (* = sentences)

1 Chronicles	29:10–13	192
Psalm	67:4*	15
	105:1*	2
Proverbs	8:22–36	180
Isaiah	9:2–7	195
	60:1–3.11.14.18–19	197
	61:10–11	194
Jeremiah	14:9	168
	7:13–14	149
Daniel	9:9*	11
Zephaniah	3:14–15	151
Matthew	10:43–49	148
	11:28–30	166
	25:34–41	146
	28:20*	5
Luke	1:46–55	185
	1:68–79	174
	2:29–32	186
	9:57–62	145
	10:21–22	163
John	11:25*	1
	13:12–17	147
	13:34*	3
	15:14–17	144
Acts	1:8*	4
Romans	5:1–8	189
	5:4–8	157
	5:5*	15
	6:3.4*	7
	6:5–14	157
	8:37–39	189
1 Corinthians	4:5*	9
	15:12–15a	142
Galatians	1:3–5	158
	6:14*	12
Ephesians	2:19–21	164
	4:25–27*	17
	4:29–32	143
Philippians	2:5–11	179
	3:8–11	159
Colossians	1:13–20	188
	3:12–15	153
	2:9–12	160
	1:9b–13	161
1 Thessalonians	5:9–10	170
1 Timothy	1:15–16	154
	2:21b–24b	155
Titus	2:11–13	152
	3:4–7	162
Hebrews	4:9–11a	171
	4:14.16*	14
1 Peter	1:3*	13
	2:24*	6
	5:8–9	167
1 John	4:9*	10
	4:9–12	150
Jude	1:24–25	169
Revelation	2:5–7	191
	5:9–10	183
	7:9–11	183
	11:17–18	190
	12:10–12	190
	15:3–4	181
	19:1	191
	22:9.5	165

INDEX OF SUBJECTS AND SEASONS

Advent 8, 55, 80, 123, 135, 149, 172, 195, 197
Ascension 13, 61, 77, 89, 105, 107, 110, 114, 118, 121, 124, 135, 161, 178, 192
Baptism 7, 47, 48, 57, 160
Church 65, 177
Creation 73, 74, 95, 96, 105, 107, 114, 127, 128, 135, 172, 175, 176, 180, 192, 198
Death 1, 101, 120, 126, 134, 165
Easter *see* Resurrection
Evening 48, 49, 52, 53, 98, 99, 101, 185, 187
Faith 13, 91, 104, 121, 134
Holy Spirit 4, 14, 45, 62, 73, 76, 90, 97, 112, 116, 133, 162
Hope 5, 33, 136
Incarnation:
   Christmas 9, 56, 81, 82, 92, 113, 117, 118, 125, 132, 150, 195
   Epiphany 57, 83, 109, 117, 135, 137, 151, 152
Judgement 8, 41, 55, 109, 117, 122, 152, 172, 190
Kingdom of God 70, 120, 126, 145, 164, 165, 177
Lent 10, 58, 84, 111, 119, 136, 153, 154, 182
Love and Service 3, 34, 44, 52, 68, 71, 144, 146, 147, 153
Morning 41–47, 75, 79, 172, 174
Night Prayer 16, 17, 39, 40, 50, 51, 54, 72, 99, 100, 102, 103, 138–141, 165–171, 186
Passion of Christ, Passiontide 11, 37, 46, 53, 59, 85, 86, 130, 131, 155, 156–158, 179
Peace 16, 17, 49, 51, 68, 69, 153
Penitence and forgiveness 10, 17, 35, 58, 69, 108, 111, 136, 137, 143, 153
Pentecost *see* Holy Spirit
Praise 12, 36, 78, 108, 114, 118, 123–125, 135, 137, 172, 174–177, 181, 183, 184, 191–194, 196
Protection from evil 39, 40, 42, 43, 50, 54, 100, 102–104, 106, 112, 115, 129, 137–140
Resurrection 12, 60, 73, 87, 88, 104, 123, 129, 142, 159, 160, 173, 183
Saints 66, 67, 93, 94, 164
Salvation in Christ 6, 7, 37, 48, 64, 142, 148, 157, 159, 188, 189, 196
Suffering 66, 156
Thanksgiving 2, 38, 113, 127, 128, 132, 133, 185
Trinity 15, 63, 73, 91, 163